The
Happy Heart
Cookbook

14.II.'05

from one happy heart to
another! ♡M

The Happy Heart Cookbook

Irish Heart Foundation

IRISH
HEART
FOUNDATION
FORAS CROI NA hEIREANN

Gill & Macmillan

Gill & Macmillan Ltd
Hume Avenue
Park West
Dublin 12
with associated companies throughout the world
www.gillmacmillan.ie
© The Irish Heart Foundation 2000
0 7171 3052 5
Index compiled by Helen Litton
Design by Slick Fish Design
Printed by ColourBooks Ltd, Dublin

Photography by Mike O'Toole
Table-ware supplied by Brown Thomas
Table-linen supplied by Bottom Drawer at Brown Thomas

A catalogue record is available for this book from the
British Library.

This book is typeset in 9 point Avenir on 14 point leading.

1 3 5 4 2

Contents

Recipes

Soups & Starters

Salads & Dressings

Fish

Meat

Poultry

Foreword

This Irish Heart Foundation cookbook is the realisation of a long-held ambition and the timing is perfect! Never before has there been as strong an interest in eating, cooking and enjoying food.

The Happy Heart Cookbook *is for people who want to eat healthily, rather than for those already on special heart health diets. It is part of our philosophy for a happy heart — enjoy food that is low in fat, low in calories, high in fibre and rich in taste. This, together with regular physical activity and not smoking, is the recipe for a healthy heart.*

This cookbook offers something a bit different. It is ideal for people who enjoy delicious food, but don't want to spend too much time cooking. Try these recipes at weekends, when life is less busy and there is time to relax and enjoy the delicious tastes. Hopefully, too, it will inspire both regular cooks and beginners.

Paddy Murphy
Chief Executive
Irish Heart Foundation

Introduction

The current interest in living well and enjoying a more relaxed, flexible lifestyle is reflected in the recent influx of magazines on lifestyle, house and home, and food. The food we eat has suddenly become as fashionable as what we wear, what we buy for our homes and the colourful plates we serve the food on.

It is all about creating an atmosphere of relaxation, sharing and enjoyment. Fresh ingredients, a simple meal, the pleasure of sharing it with family and friends — that is today's idea of good food.

The luxury of little cherry tomatoes grown in your garden, a bunch of basil leaves picked from your window-sill, a home-made dressing and some oven-warmed bread — delicious, and good enough to transport you to some sun-drenched terrace in the Mediterranean!

This cookbook is really about enjoying and sharing good food. Food simply prepared, with light dressings and sauces that allow you to taste the real flavour. The fact that the dishes are good for your heart and your shape is an added bonus.

Enjoy good health. Nurture and relax your body. Do not take it for granted.

Acknowledgments

A number of people have been invaluable in the development of this first Happy Heart Cookbook. *Ursula O'Dwyer, consultant dietitian to the Irish Heart Foundation for many years, carefully selected and developed the recipes and compiled the healthy eating section.*

The recipes were meticulously tested by Honor Moore and Biddy White Lennon, both food writers and members of the Irish Food Writers Guild. Honor and Biddy were more than generous with their time, energy and suggestions and provided recipes for the section on vegetables. Mike O'Toole provided the beautiful photography with help from food stylist and chef Anne Marie Tobin.

Brown Thomas supplied the table-ware and Bottom Drawer at Brown Thomas the table-linen.

Several staff in the Irish Heart Foundation played a key role in this project. Aoibheann O'Connor, dietitian, and Maureen Mulvihill, health promotion manager, provided excellent input at all stages of the book. Thanks also to the staff in the Health Promotion Department who helped with typing and proofing.

The Irish Heart Foundation also acknowledges the enthusiasm and support from Gill & Macmillan and from Eveleen Coyle in particular. It is most encouraging to have the expertise and interest of such an established publisher for this first publication.

Healthy Living

Good health, relaxation, comfort, nurture, friendship and love — these are all elements of good living.

Caught up with the demands of work and domestic life, we live in an environment that demands our immediate reaction to every ring of the phone, fax transmission or e-mail. It is important to find some quiet time and to have some space for yourself away from family, friends and work. Find a simple retreat, a peaceful spot in the garden, a favourite chair near a south-facing window or a quiet walk.

Taking time out for yourself, especially if you have a family, is a learned behaviour and not one that comes naturally. Yet it is one of the most important behaviours for healthy living. It helps reduce the build-up of stress, which is now known to be a contributing risk for coronary heart disease.

Take time out to do simple things:
- Enjoy your garden: both the exercise and the fresh air will help to lift your spirits.
- Spend time playing with your children; enjoy a shower of rain together!
- While working, let the gentle strings of classical music soothe your busy mind.
- Enjoy the fruits of your labour, even if it is just herbs grown on a window ledge.
- Have a walk: being outdoors invigorates the senses.
- Look around you and keep in touch with nature.
- Walk barefoot on the grass or — even better — on the beach or in the sea.
- Enjoy lazy lunches in the garden.
- Share good food with friends and family.

Living well means enjoying good food, good health and healthy eating. It means having days for parties and meals out and balancing these with days of light eating.

It means most days using the Food Pyramid as a guide and following the Ten Easy Steps for Reducing Fat (see page 21). It is about having a healthy respect for your body and what you put into it. It is about taking regular physical activity and maintaining a level of fitness that keeps you feeling young and energetic. It is about making the best of what you have, enjoying life and being happy.

Take time out to smell the roses!

Each ▲ is one serving.
The number of servings needed each day for adults is shown on the Food Pyramid.
Start on the bottom shelf of the Pyramid and choose more of these foods than those from the top shelf. Servings in each group are interchangeable.

For example to get at least four servings from the fruit and vegetable shelf you could have:

½ glass of fruit juice	*= 1*
1 portion of vegetables	*= 1*
1 apple	*= 1*
1 banana	*= 1*
	4

**Drink water regularly —
at least eight cups of
fluid per day**

sparingly

2 servings

3 servings

4+ servings

6+ servings

Folic Acid — *an essential ingredient in making a baby.*
You can get Folic Acid from green leafy vegetables but if there is any possibility that you could become pregnant then you should be taking a Folic Acid tablet (400 micrograms per day).

others

Fats and oils Use about 1 oz low-fat spread/low-fat butter or ¹/₂ oz margarine/butter. Use oils sparingly. Ovenbake foods instead of frying or deep fat frying.

Sugars, confectionery, cakes, biscuits and high-fat snack foods If you drink or eat snacks containing sugar, limit the number of times you take them throughout the day. Eat high-fat snacks only in small amounts and not too frequently.
Choose low-fat, sugar-free alternatives.

Alcohol In moderation, preferably with meals — and have some alcohol-free days.

meat, fish and alternatives

Choose two of the following each day —
choose three servings during pregnancy

▲ 2 oz cooked lean meat or poultry
▲ 3 oz cooked fish
▲ 2 eggs (not more than seven per week)
▲ 6 tablespoons cooked peas/beans
▲ 2 oz cheddar-type cheese (preferably low-fat)
▲ 3 oz nuts

milk, cheese and yoghurt

Choose any three of the following each day

▲ ¹/₃ pint of milk
▲ 1 carton of yoghurt
▲ 1 oz cheddar cheese or Blarney/Edam

Choose low-fat choices frequently (not suitable for young children). Low-fat milk is not suitable for children under two years of age. Choose at least four servings for teenagers. Choose five servings for pregnant and breast-feeding women.

fruit and vegetables

Choose at least four or more of the following
each day

▲ ¹/₂ glass of fruit juice
▲ 1 medium sized fresh fruit
▲ 2 tablespoons cooked vegetables or salad
▲ small bowl of homemade vegetable soup
▲ 2 tablespoons cooked fruit or tinned fruit

Choose citrus fruits and fruit juices frequently

bread, cereals and potatoes

Choose at least six or more of the following
each day

▲ 1 bowl of breakfast cereal
▲ 1 slice of bread
▲ 2 tablespoons of cooked pasta or rice
▲ 1 medium potato boiled or baked

Choose high-fibre cereals and breads frequently.
If physical activity is high up to 12 servings may be needed.

Why Heart Healthy Eating

To get the most out of life, it is important to take care of our bodies and to take responsibility for the food we eat. What we eat may make the difference between good quality and enjoyment of life and an early death.

This section explains the often confusing relationship between what we eat, especially fats, and heart disease.

All food is good — balance is the key

No one food is good or bad; it is the overall daily and weekly balance of foods which determines whether a diet or eating plan is healthy or not.

The cornerstones of healthy eating are having plenty of variety and getting the balance right, a balance between getting enough essential nutrients without getting too much of any one nutrient, particularly one like fat.

It is more difficult to have a healthy diet if we eat only a limited number of foods, particularly if those foods are high in fat and low in fibre. As wide a variety of different foods as possible is more likely to provide all the nutrients needed.

To eat a wide variety of foods, follow the servings guide on the Food Pyramid.

Fat and Cholesterol

Fat and cholesterol have a very important role in relation to heart health.

Fat acts as an insulator, protects joints, vital organs, such as the kidneys, and is a source of energy. It also provides the fat-soluble vitamins A, D and E and essential fatty acids.

High-fat foods eaten regularly, especially foods that are high in saturated fat, tend to raise blood cholesterol levels. As blood cholesterol goes up, so do the chances of having a heart attack or a stroke.

One change in eating habits — lowering the amount of total fat and saturated fat — would be a good action to take for heart health.

Look around you and keep in touch with nature.

Confused about Dietary Fat?

There are different types of fat in food — saturated, monounsaturated and polyunsaturated. Each type has a different effect on blood cholesterol level.

Although we tend to think of dietary fat as being one type, it is actually a mixture of all three types of fat. However, it is common practice to describe a food according to the type of fat present in the largest amount. For example, butter is generally referred to as a saturated fat although it contains as much as 30% monounsaturated and 4% polyunsaturated fat.

Saturated Fats

Saturated fats tend to raise blood cholesterol. As a nation, Irish people are eating too much saturated fat in proportion to the other food fats, which explains why cutting down on foods containing saturated fats is important. Most of the saturated fat comes from animal foods like meat, meat products, milk, butter and foods made with hydrogenated vegetable oils like hard margarine, cakes, biscuits and pastries. Hydrogenated vegetable oils are also used widely in confectionery and in deep-fried foods.

Polyunsaturated Fats

Polyunsaturated fats can help to lower blood cholesterol. These fats are found mainly in vegetable oils such as sunflower, safflower, corn, soya bean, and sesame oil and some nuts like walnuts, hazelnuts, Brazil nuts and pine nuts. Oily fish such as mackerel, herring, trout, salmon and sardines are also rich sources of polyunsaturated fats.

Monounsaturated Fats

These fats may also have a lowering effect on blood cholesterol when substituted for saturated fats. They are found in many of the fats we eat regularly. However, the most concentrated source of these fats is in vegetable oils, such as olive, peanut and rapeseed oil, as well as in avocados, seeds and some nuts, for example, cashew, almonds and peanuts.

The total amount of fat eaten is important, so we need to limit all types of fat, especially saturated fat. Oils are the *most* concentrated source of fat and they should be used sparingly.

Healthy Fat Intake for a Day (Department of Health and Children)

Average Woman (19–64 yrs)	Average Man (19–64 yrs)
74–97 g fat per day	93–128 g fat per day
roughly equivalent to: (1 teaspoon = 5 g fat approx.)	
15–19 teaspoons of fat	19–26 teaspoons of fat

The lower limit should be the target if overweight or there is a family history of heart disease.

Although many foods contain fat, most of the fat we eat comes from five main sources:

- All fried and deep fat-fried foods. Many fast foods and snack foods will fall into this category e.g. crisps.
- Butter, margarine, low-fat spreads (half the fat of butter/margarine), mayonnaise, oils and salad dressings, cream, sour cream and ice-cream.
- Cakes, biscuits, chocolates and other high-fat foods on the top shelf of the Food Pyramid.
- Fatty meats and meat products such as beefburgers and sausages.
- Full-fat dairy products like full-fat milk, cheese and full-fat yoghurts.

Fat Facts

- A teaspoon of butter, margarine or oil is equivalent to approximately 5 g of fat. This means that as much as 10 g of fat could be saved on a sandwich.
- All oils are almost 100% fat, including olive oil. A good non-stick pan helps to start foods off with very little or no fat at all. A non-stick low-fat spray is available in most supermarkets or an oil spray that allows the minimum amount of oil to be used.
- Switching from whole milk to low-fat milk can save as much as 1 g of fat in every cup of tea or coffee — that's 6 g or more a day.
- Using a low-fat/fat-free dressing can reduce fat intake by up to 12 g on a salad.
- Smaller portions of meat, fish and poultry (about a 90 g/3½ oz serving) can reduce fat intake. A 3½ oz portion of *lean* beef, pork or lamb has about 9 g of fat; poultry (without skin) about 5 g of fat; oily fish like salmon about 7 g of fat and white fish like cod 2 g of fat.
- Regular cheese eaters could try grated low-fat cheddar instead of full-fat cheese, especially in cooking, on toast or in toasted or plain sandwiches. A strong dressing such as wholegrain mustard offers an alternative zest and taste. By choosing 2 oz of low-fat cheddar in preference to full-fat cheddar, 9 g of fat can be saved.

Cholesterol Facts

- People are often confused when they read or hear about cholesterol. There are two types of cholesterol — blood cholesterol and dietary cholesterol.
- Blood cholesterol is a type of fat produced naturally by the liver and is part of cells in the body. Cholesterol is needed for a healthy nervous system, good digestion and to produce important hormones — our bodies could not function without it.
- Dietary cholesterol, on the other hand, is the cholesterol found in foods, such as egg yolks, offal (liver, kidney) shellfish and fish roe. Many people believe that cholesterol in foods is primarily responsible for raising blood cholesterol, but we now know that dietary cholesterol does not effect blood cholesterol nearly as much as dietary fat, particularly saturated fat, as this converts to cholesterol in the body. Foods rich in cholesterol are in fact only eaten in small amounts compared to foods high in saturated fats.
- In terms of healthy eating, the amount of total fat and saturated fat in foods eaten *regularly* deserves far more attention than foods that are rich in cholesterol.

The Good and the Bad Blood Cholesterol

The relationship between blood cholesterol and heart disease is very complex, but it helps to understand how blood cholesterol travels through the body. To transport blood cholesterol to the various cells, it is combined with a 'carrier protein' to form fat/protein mixtures called lipoproteins.

There are two main forms of lipoprotein

- LDL cholesterol (low density lipoprotein) often called 'bad' cholesterol
- HDL cholesterol (high density lipoprotein) often called 'good' cholesterol

HDL cholesterol seems to protect against heart disease by clearing or 'mopping up' cholesterol from the arteries. People who exercise regularly, non-smokers, pre-menopausal women and moderate drinkers are more likely to have higher HDL cholesterol.

The blood cholesterol that you do not want too much of is the LDL cholesterol, as it gets deposited or 'left behind' along the arteries, clogging them up and increasing the risk of a heart attack.

To reduce the risk of coronary heart disease, it is important to keep LDL cholesterol levels as low as possible and HDL as high as possible. Choosing fats with care and taking regular physical activity will help you achieve this balance.

Fibre-rich Foods

Bread, cereals, potatoes, pasta and rice are starchy foods which are high in carbohydrate. That means they provide energy over a longer period of time, are very nutritious providing minerals and vitamins, and are naturally low in fat. They are high in fibre, more naturally filling and keep the bowels working properly.

It is important to eat more of these foods which are rich in starch and fibre. Eating starchy foods, especially wholegrain varieties, provides energy and fibre. Research indicates that when increased amounts of these foods are eaten, a lower fat intake can be maintained more successfully.

By basing meals primarily on these foods and eating protein foods such as meat, fish, cheese and eggs in smaller amounts, it is easier to keep fat intake at a healthy level and to eat more fibre.

Soluble Fibre

Soluble fibre is a soft fibre that seems to help in the control of blood sugar levels and in lowering LDL cholesterol levels, especially if they are higher than average. Oat bran and oat-based cereals, together with peas, beans and lentils, fruits rich in pectin such as apples, strawberries and citrus fruits, and barley are the best sources of soluble fibre.

Insoluble Fibre

This type of fibre helps to prevent and control bowel problems and may be important in preventing certain cancers. The best sources are wheatbran and wheat or bran-based cereals, wholegrain foods like wholemeal bread, fruit and vegetables including skins and seeds when appropriate.

While working, let the gentle strings of classical music soothe your busy mind.

Vegetables and Fruit

Medical and scientific evidence now suggests that a high fruit and vegetable intake is associated with a reduced risk of developing heart disease because of the antioxidant vitamin content of vegetables and fruit.

Increasing vegetable and fruit intake to four or more portions every day is one of the most important and easiest healthy eating habits to develop.

What are antioxidant vitamins and minerals?

These are vitamins that prevent oxygen from doing damage in our bodies — a similar process occurs when a peeled apple is left exposed to the atmosphere. These vitamins are vitamin A, vitamin C, vitamin E, or ACE vitamins. Vitamin A is found in dark green leafy vegetables, yellow and orange vegetables and yellow and orange fruit; vitamin C in vegetables, most fruits, especially citrus fruits and their juices; and vitamin E in vegetable oil, especially sunflower oil, nuts and seeds.

Citrus fruits and juices, orange vegetables and dark green leafy vegetables should be enjoyed at least every other day to provide enough antioxidants.

In general it is considered better to eat increasing amounts of vegetables and fruit rather than take vitamin supplements.

A Healthy Weight

Good health depends on having a healthy body weight, being neither too thin nor too fat, but falling within a weight range which is suitable for a particular body build. From a heart health point of view this is important because overweight people are at greater risk of developing high blood pressure, raised blood cholesterol and diabetes, all risk factors for heart disease and stroke.

Energy in (as food) and energy out (as activity) needs to be balanced for a healthy weight. The Food Pyramid is a guide for food choices and it is important to include at least 30 minutes or more of physical activity on most, if not every, day in the week.

To lose weight, it is best to follow a low-fat healthy eating plan combined with regular exercise. Dieting does not work. 'Going on a diet' for a month, three months or six months means that you 'come off' the diet after that length of time, revert to your old eating habits and put back on the weight that you lost.

Current research suggests that the most effective way to lose weight and keep weight off is to follow a low-fat healthy eating plan and include 30–60 minutes of exercise most days of the week.

Sugar

Sugar provides energy with minimal amounts of vitamins, minerals and fibre.

A mixture of starchy foods and some sugary foods may help make low-fat eating more palatable and easier to maintain in the long term.

It is recommended that sugars such as table sugar, jam, honey, biscuits, confectionery and sugary drinks should be chosen less frequently. The likelihood of tooth decay is increased by the frequency of eating these foods. However, if these foods are eaten as part of a balanced meal, then there is less chance of tooth decay occurring.

Salt

Current evidence suggests that salt (sodium chloride/NaCl) intake contributes to the increase in blood pressure, which occurs as people get older, and is one of the main causes of heart disease.

Eating less salt, both in pre-prepared or processed foods and in cooking, is important for heart health. In general, a third of salt intake comes from salty foods like ham and salty snack foods like crisps; another third comes from tinned and processed foods like soups and sauces; and a final third we add ourselves in cooking or at meals.

Often people forget the 'hidden' salt in prepared, convenience foods and snack foods.

Herbs, spices, lemon juice, black pepper and garlic can be used as alternative flavourings to salt. In addition to reducing salt intake, increasing fruit, vegetables and wholegrain starchy foods may help to control blood pressure, as they are good sources of potassium.

Salt substitutes can be useful in helping to reduce salt intake, but they still contain sodium and may not be suitable for people with renal or cardiac disorders. Onion salt, garlic salt and sea salt all contain sodium and are of little benefit in lowering sodium intake. Dried foods contain a lot of salt. On labels watch out for words like 'sodium' and 'monosodium glutamate' — they all mean salt.

Alcohol

Those who drink small amounts of alcohol on a regular basis may have a reduced risk of heart disease. This means no more than 2–3 drinks a day, with some days in the week free of alcohol.

Excess alcohol intake raises blood pressure (a risk factor for coronary heart disease and stroke), increases the risk of some cancers and contributes to overweight.

Recommended Upper Limit for Drinking Alcohol

Men	21 units a week
Women	14 units a week
1 glass of beer or wine	= 1 unit
1 measure of spirits	= 1.5 units

Enjoy lazy lunches in the garden.

Heart Healthy Eating Guidelines

Based on medical evidence, the following guidelines have been drawn up by both the Irish Heart Foundation and the Health Promotion Unit, Department of Health and Children. In fact, in 1996 the key health and medical groups in Ireland produced a Consensus Statement to endorse these guidelines.

These guidelines promote and maintain good health, which also helps in reducing the risk of heart disease. The way to heart healthy eating is to:

- Eat a wide variety of foods
- Maintain a healthy weight
- Eat less fat, especially saturated fats
- Eat more bread, cereals, potatoes, pasta and rice
- Eat more vegetables and fruit
- Choose sugary foods and drinks less often
- Eat less salt
- If you drink alcohol, keep within sensible limits

Healthy eating is only one component of a healthy lifestyle — not smoking, regular exercise, occasional blood pressure and cholesterol checks and developing coping strategies for dealing with stress are also important.

Share good food with family and friends.

Cooking for Health

A healthy diet isn't simply determined by the foods we eat. The way these foods are prepared and cooked can have a significant effect on their nutritional value.

A recent survey commissioned by the Irish Heart Foundation found that only 22% of those surveyed recognised the importance of how meals are cooked. The remaining 78% focused mainly on the food itself — for example, eating more fruit and vegetables rather than avoiding cooking methods which add fat, such as frying — the age old tradition in Ireland.

The way food is cooked *is* important. Take a healthy food like a potato. A boiled or baked potato has almost no fat, but a portion of chips has 22 g of fat.

The recent popularity of olive oil is an example of confusion about cooking and health. There is a perception that using several tablespoons to start off a dish is healthy; but all oils, including olive oil, are almost 100% fat. Reducing *total* fat intake as well as your intake of saturated fat is important.

Here are some suggestions for healthier cooking methods.

Grilling

Grilling is an excellent way of cooking meat, fish, poultry, and some vegetables. It requires little or no fat to be added during cooking and is therefore a much healthier alternative to frying. Marinating food before grilling will improve the flavour and help tenderise meat. Food can be left in the marinade for at least one hour before cooking, or preferably overnight, covered and in the fridge, for some types of marinade.

Grilling is a good method for cooking oily fish such as mackerel, salmon and trout. Mushrooms, tomatoes and other vegetables can also be grilled successfully. Mushrooms may need to be brushed lightly with a little oil first and cooked under a moderate grill.

Roasting

This is a healthy way of cooking meat, poultry and root vegetables. Ideally, the joint or bird is placed on the rack, over a roasting tin, so that the fat drips underneath. Fat is drained off before using the remaining juices to make gravy.

Roasting is an excellent way to cook peppers, onions, courgettes, garlic and parsnips. Vegetables are cut into large chunks, blanched in boiling water and thoroughly drained, then placed in a roasting tin with low edges. Half a tablespoon of olive oil is drizzled over the vegetables. The vegetables are well tossed, then seasoned with freshly ground pepper and cooked in a moderate oven until tender.

Halved tomatoes or cherry tomatoes can also be roasted. No blanching or oil is needed, but dusting with chopped garlic or herbs will add flavour.

Stir-frying

Stir-fried food has a good texture and flavour. It is a quick method of cooking and helps to preserve the vitamins as well as the flavour of the vegetables used. Stir-frying uses less fat than shallow frying.

All the vegetables need to be cut into even-sized pieces so that they cook in the same amount of time. Use a wok or a deep-sided frying pan. The oil must be really hot before adding all the ingredients. Spoon in a little water if the vegetables start to stick.

Boiling

Boiling is an excellent way of cooking vegetables. To ensure that the water-soluble vitamins present in vegetables (in particular vitamin C) are not lost during boiling, vegetables should be added to a small amount of boiling water and cooked for as short a time as possible until they are just tender but still have some 'bite'. Retain some of the water-soluble vitamins which remain in the vegetable water to make gravy, stock or soup.

Steaming

Steaming is one of the best methods of cooking vegetables. It helps to retain their flavour, colour and most importantly the water-soluble vitamins, which are easily lost during other cooking methods. Other foods such as fish and poultry can also be steamed.

Walk barefoot on the grass.

Stewing

This slow method of cooking is ideal for tenderising tougher cuts of meat. The meat is cooked with vegetables and flavourings and just enough liquid to cover them. If they are made the day before, stews and casseroles can be quickly cooled, refrigerated and then any excess fat can be removed easily from the surface before being reheated. Cooking the day before also has the advantage of adding depth to the flavour.

Microwave Cooking

Microwaves cook food very quickly and without the need to add extra fat or large amounts of fat. This way of cooking helps to retain vitamins, particularly the water-soluble vitamins (B vitamins and vitamin C) that can be easily destroyed by other cooking methods.

Microwave cooking is particularly useful for cooking vegetables and fish and for defrosting and reheating food quickly.

See what a difference cooking methods make by looking at the figures below.

Average Potato Portion	Grams of fat	Calories
Boiled (175 g)	0.18 g	126 kcal
Baked (180 g)	0.36 g	244 kcal
Mashed (3 scoops 180 g, no butter, a little milk)	0.54 g	120 kcal
Mashed (3 scoops 180 g, with butter)	8.5 g	187 kcal
Roast (200 g, with blended oil)	9 g	298 kcal
Chips (165 g straight cut, in blended oil)	22.2 g	450 kcal

Enjoy your garden. Both the exercise and the fresh air will help to lift your spirits.

▼ Pork with Mango Salsa (page 58)

◀ Mixed Red Berry Sorbet (page 103)

▼ Carrot Cake (page 112)

◀ Raspberry and Cinnamon Meringue (page 101)

▼ Spicy Parsnip and Apple Soup (page 25)

Buffalo Mozzarella with Vine Tomatoes and Basil (page 38) ▶

Chinese Turkey Kebabs with Noodles and Beansprouts (page 68) ▶

Cooking Guidelines

Low-fat Healthy Dish

- To make a low-fat healthy dish, little or no oil or fat should be used in cooking.
- Use low-fat cooking methods — steam, grill, poach, microwave, oven bake, stir-fry or dry roast.
- All fat should be trimmed from meat. Order lean meat from your butcher. Pre-cook mince and drain off fat for mince-based dishes.
- Cook chicken without skin, where possible.
- Use low-fat or light mayonnaise in coleslaw and other salad dressings requiring mayonnaise.
- Serve dressings and sauces separately.
- Use low-fat milk and low-fat cheese in cooking.

Vegetables

- Always wash fruit and vegetables. To save vitamins do not peel, if possible.
- Prepare vegetables just before cooking as cutting or chopping speeds up the loss of vitamins.
- If fresh vegetables must be prepared early, rather than soaking in water, cover with a lid or with tin foil and put in the fridge, as this reduces vitamin loss. Steaming vegetables will also help to reduce vitamin loss.
- When stir-frying vegetables, use oil sparingly.
- Go for some salad choices without dressings.
- Go for lower-fat dressings — light mayonnaise, reduced calorie salad cream or low fat vinaigrette.

Fruit

- A tasty low-fat healthy dessert option is an attractive fruit plate or fruit salad.
- Go for a variety of fruit juices, especially orange and grapefruit.
- Tasty and healthy toppings for fruit dishes are low-fat custard, low-fat yoghurt, low-fat fromage frais or a little light cream.
- Try fruit ice or sorbet or frozen yoghurt instead of ice-cream.

Enjoy the fruits of your labour, even if it is just herbs grown on a window ledge.

Ten Easy Steps for Reducing Fat

Choose Wisely

- Eat less foods from the top shelf of the Food Pyramid — less oils, less fats, fewer cakes, biscuits, chocolates, less savoury snacks like crisps.

Cut the Spread on Bread

- Spread butter or margarine sparingly.
- Switch to a low-fat spread and use thinly.
- Choose a polyunsaturated or monounsaturated spread. Try different types to find one that you like best.

Use Less Fat in Cooking

- Grill, oven bake, steam, stew, casserole or microwave without added fat or oils — don't fry.
- Measure out oil rather than pouring on to the pan.
- Spice up your life! Instead of fat, add herbs, spices, lemon juice, garlic, onion, ginger and black pepper to your food.

Go for Low-fat Mayonnaise or Dressings

- Try fat-free dressing, light mayonnaise and reduced-fat salad cream in small amounts.
- Use ordinary mayonnaise, salad cream or French dressing sparingly.

Choose Snack Food Low in Fat

- Choose fruit instead of high-fat foods such as cake, biscuits, chocolates, pastries and crisps.
- Offer cereal with milk as a between meal or bedtime snack.

Check the Label Before You Buy Convenience Food

- Look for the lower-fat choice.
- Check the label for: butter, margarine, oil (vegetable or hydrogenated), cream, suet, shortening, cocoa butter and lard.
- Remember the higher these are on the ingredient list, the more fat in the product.

Lean Towards Low-fat Meats

- Choose lean meat and trim off fat before cooking.
- Remove skin from chicken before cooking.
- Eat more fish, a naturally low-fat food.
- Bake, don't fry breaded fish and chicken as these already contain added fat.

Choose Low-fat Dairy Products Often

- Cook with low-fat milk and cheese, but give full-fat milk to young children.
- Milk is a valuable food and shouldn't be given up. Drink full-fat milk if you don't like low-fat.
- Top your desserts with low-fat custards and low-fat yoghurts.

Eat More Fruit and Vegetables

- Choose more fruit and vegetables which are ideal low-fat foods.
- Try eating fruits and/or vegetables at every meal.
- Snack on fruit and raw vegetables rather than high-fat foods like crisps, biscuits and cakes.
- Get into the habit of adding tomato, lettuce or cucumber to sandwiches.
- Eat in season. Salad-based meals such as tuna, ham or cheese are delicious.

Eat More Bread, Cereals and Potatoes

- Enjoy breads, cereals and potatoes which are low in fats.
- Eat with main meals and/or as snacks.
- Choose high-fibre breads and cereals frequently.
- Ring the changes — choose rolls, crispbreads, pitta pockets and savoury breads.

The above is taken from the *Go for Low Fat Healthy Eating* magazine, National Healthy Eating campaign 1998, produced by the Department of Health and Children.

Soups & Starters

Spicy Parsnip and Apple Soup

Starchy root vegetables like parsnips are very good value in season and make delicious filling soup. This soup with added apple and curry flavouring is real 'comfort' food! Enjoy as a light lunch or starter.

What you need:

- 450 g/1 lb parsnips, peeled
- 225 g/8 oz apples, peeled
- 1 onion, finely chopped
- 15 ml/1 tablespoon olive oil
- 1 level tablespoon mild curry powder
- 600 ml/1 pint vegetable stock
- 300 ml/¾ pint low-fat milk
- 2 teaspoons cumin seeds to garnish (optional)
- a little salt and freshly ground black pepper

Preparation:	10 minutes
Cooking:	30 minutes
Freezing:	yes
Serves:	4

What you do:

Divide the parsnips in half and remove the woody stems. Cut the parsnips and apples into even-sized pieces. Heat the oil in a heavy-based saucepan, add the vegetables and stir. Cover and cook for a few minutes until the vegetables are slightly softened. Sprinkle in the curry powder and cook, stirring for one minute. Stir in the vegetable stock and the milk and season with a little salt and pepper. Bring to the boil, then reduce the heat to a gentle simmer and cook for 15 minutes until the vegetables are soft. Allow the soup to cool a little, then transfer to a liquidiser and liquidise until smooth. If the consistency is a little too thick for your liking, add a little more milk or vegetable stock.

If using cumin seeds, place a small pan over a medium heat and toast the seeds for a minute or two (until they darken but not burn). Meanwhile, return the soup to the saucepan and reheat gently. Serve the soup in warmed soup bowls garnished with a sprinkling of cumin seeds if used.

Per Serving	
Calories	181 kcal
Fat	7 g
Saturated Fat	1.5 g
Fibre	7 g

Carrot
and Coriander Soup

A favourite combination — coriander brings out the carrot flavour in this soup. Carrots are rich in carotene (vitamin A) and have important antioxidant benefits that help protect against heart disease — so eat plenty!

What you need:

- 8 large carrots, chopped
- 1 onion, chopped
- 1 medium potato, peeled and chopped
- 10–12 coriander seeds, crushed
- 500 ml/12 fl oz vegetable stock
- 4 sprays frying oil spray
- freshly chopped parsley for garnish
- a little salt and freshly ground black pepper

Preparation:	10 minutes
Cooking:	30 minutes
Freezing:	yes (10 days approx.)
Serves:	4

What you do:

Heat a heavy saucepan, spray 4 times with oil spray and add the onion and coriander seeds. Season with a little salt and freshly ground black pepper, cover and cook gently for about 3–4 minutes. Add the vegetable stock, carrots and potatoes, cover and bring to the boil, then simmer for 20 minutes. Liquidise and return to the saucepan and heat through. Serve with freshly chopped parsley.

Note: 'Frying oil sprays' coat saucepans with a very fine misting of oil, making meals low in fat and calories.

Per Serving	
Calories	142 kcal
Fat	1 g
Saturated Fat	0.2 g
Fibre	7.8 g

Gazpacho/Spanish Tomato Soup

This Mediterranean cold soup makes a delicious light summer lunch or starter.
Tomatoes used as the base for this soup and many recipes in this book are an easy way
to add health-boosting vitamins A and C (antioxidant vitamins) to meals.

What you need:

- 4 thick slices white bread, crusts removed
- 2–3 cloves garlic, crushed, peeled and finely chopped
- 600 g/1¼ lb ripe tomatoes, peeled and deseeded
- 350 ml/12 fl oz chilled water
- 2 red peppers, trimmed, deseeded and roughly chopped
- 1 small cucumber, peeled, deseeded and roughly chopped
- 1 small red onion, peeled and chopped
- 350 g/12 oz tinned tomatoes, chopped
- 4 tablespoons sherry vinegar or red wine vinegar
- 1 tablespoon extra virgin olive oil (optional)
- ½ teaspoon fresh mint, chopped
- Tabasco sauce to taste
- a little salt and freshly ground black pepper

Garnishes:

- 1 small red pepper, deseeded and diced
- 3 firm ripe tomatoes, peeled, deseeded and diced
- ½ small cucumber, peeled, deseeded and diced
- 1 small red onion, peeled and finely chopped
- finely chopped parsley or mint

Preparation:	35 minutes
Cooking:	none
Freezing:	yes (without added bread)
Serves:	6

What you do:

Tear the bread into pieces and reduce to crumbs in a food processor with the garlic. Sieve the fresh tomatoes into a bowl to remove the pips. (Omit this stage for a rustic version.) Add sufficient water to make up to 450 ml/¾ pint. Put the peppers, onion, cucumber, mint and tomatoes into the food processor and blend until fairly smooth. Combine with the vinegar, Tabasco, salt and pepper to taste, plus a spoonful of olive oil if desired. Arrange the garnishes in separate bowls to sprinkle over the soup at the table.

Note: The rustic version of this soup has considerable body; the 'polite' version purées and sieves the ingredients to make a smooth soup. Try it both ways and see which you prefer. It can almost be a liquid salad or, with more water added (and olive oil), a smooth creamy mixture served, with lots of ice cubes, as a soup in hot weather.

Per Serving	
Calories	223 kcal
Fat	5.7 g
Saturated Fat	0.8 g
Fibre	5.7 g

Herb and Anchovy Bruschetta

Bruschetta makes a delicious starter, especially in summer, eaten outdoors with barbecued food. Quick and easy to make, bruschetta is a delicious snack to offer with summer drinks.

What you need:

- 1 French baguette or a loaf of Italian bread cut into ½ inch slices
- 2 cloves garlic
- 75 g/3 oz (3 packets or bunches) parsley, chopped
- 6 anchovies, drained
- 1 tablespoon capers, drained
- 30 ml/2 tablespoons olive oil
- ½ red chilli, deseeded and finely chopped
- a little salt and freshly ground black pepper

Preparation:	10 minutes
Cooking:	2 minutes
Freezing:	no
Serves:	4–6

What you do:

Make a paste of anchovies, capers, chilli, parsley, olive oil and one clove of garlic by placing in a food processor and processing until you have a paste. Alternatively, pound to a paste in a mortar and pestle. Season with a little salt and freshly ground black pepper and keep cool until needed.

Toast the slices of bread on both sides. Cut the second clove of garlic in half crossways and rub the cut clove on the toasted bread. Smear the paste thinly on the hot toast and serve immediately.

Note: Tomato and basil bruschetta can be made using the same method. Skin and chop 8 plum tomatoes, add one crushed and finely chopped clove of garlic and about 8–10 leaves of basil torn into small pieces, and season with salt and freshly ground black pepper.

Per Serving	(if serving 6)	(if serving 4)
Calories	167 kcal	250 kcal
Fat	6.8 g	10 g
Saturated Fat	0.9 g	1.4 g
Fibre	2 g	3 g

Garlic Yoghurt Dip
with Crudités

This yoghurt dip is low in fat and is a delicious way to enjoy raw vegetables. Let children try it with carrot sticks and cucumber chunks.

What you need:

- 1 x 200 ml tub/7 fl oz natural or Greek yoghurt
- 1 large garlic clove, crushed
- 1 tablespoon honey
- 3 tablespoons mixed herbs, chopped — chives, parsley, basil and oregano
- a little salt and freshly ground black pepper
- 450 g/1 lb mixed crudités, such as broccoli florets, carrot sticks, radishes, cherry tomatoes, celery sticks and cucumber chunks

Preparation:	25 minutes vegetables and 2–3 hours chilling
Cooking:	none
Freezing:	no
Serves:	6

What you do:

Combine the yoghurt, garlic, herbs, honey and seasoning in a bowl. Chill for at least 2–3 hours before serving. Serve the dip accompanied by the crudités.

Per Serving	
Calories	95 kcal
Fat	5 g
Saturated Fat	2.7 g
Fibre	1.4 g

Roasted Red Peppers
with Anchovies

This starter is very tasty, quick and easy to prepare and doesn't take too long to cook. Think of all the heart-healthy antioxidant vitamins you'll be getting. Who says good food can't taste delicious?

What you need:

- 4 large red peppers, halved and deseeded
- 4 medium tomatoes, skinned and quartered
- 8 tinned anchovy fillets, drained
- 2 cloves garlic, chopped
- 8 large basil leaves, chopped
- freshly ground black pepper
- a little extra virgin olive oil

Preparation:	10 minutes
Cooking:	1 hour
Freezing:	no
Serves:	4

What you do:

On a lightly oiled baking sheet place the halved red peppers. Put 2 tomato quarters into each.

Divide the chopped garlic and basil between the peppers and roughly cut an anchovy fillet into each half pepper. Grind a little black pepper and drizzle a few drops of olive oil over each half pepper. Bake in the oven at 190°C/375°F/Gas 5 for about 1 hour.

Serve the peppers with any remaining juices poured over them and garnish with freshly chopped basil leaves. Delicious with warm crusty bread.

Per Serving
Calories	87 kcal
Fat	2.8 g
Saturated Fat	0.34 g
Fibre	3.3 g

Roasted Peppers with Fennel and Garlic

Peppers, especially red peppers, are very popular at the moment and are rich in carotene (vitamin A) and vitamin C. Roasting peppers gives them a delicious 'smokey sweet' flavour which, combined with the liquorice taste of fennel, makes this a special starter.

What you need:

- 4 large red peppers, halved and deseeded
- 2 small or 1 large fennel bulb
- 15–30 ml/1–2 tablespoons olive oil
- 1 tablespoon garlic, chopped
- 1 tablespoon onion, finely chopped
- 2 tablespoons fresh parsley, chopped
- a little salt and freshly ground black pepper

Preparation:	15 minutes
Cooking:	1 hour
Freezing:	no
Serves:	4

What you do:

Remove the pith from the peppers and place, cut side up, in a lightly greased baking tin. Keeping the layers attached to the root ends, slice the fennel lengthways into quarters and then into eighths. Boil in salted water for 5 minutes. Drain and cool. Pre-heat oven to 180°C/350°F/Gas 4. Scatter half the garlic and onion into the peppers and arrange two pieces of fennel in each half. Scatter the remaining garlic and onion over the fennel and drizzle the olive oil over the top. Bake, uncovered, for 1 hour or until tender and lightly browned. Transfer to a serving dish, spooning over any juices from the baking tin. Garnish with the parsley. Serve hot or at room temperature with bread to soak up the juices.

Per Serving	
Calories	111 kcal
Fat	8 g
Saturated Fat	1.2 g
Fibre	3 g

Roasted Vegetables with Tzatziki and Balsamic Vinegar

Tzatziki, a Greek favourite, together with a little balsamic vinegar, combines with this selection of roasted Mediterranean vegetables to give a delicious flavour.

What you need:

- 2 red onions, peeled
- 2 cloves garlic, peeled and chopped
- 1 yellow pepper, deseeded
- 1 red pepper, deseeded
- 1 small aubergine, trimmed
- 2 courgettes, trimmed
- 2 cloves garlic, peeled, crushed and chopped
- 15 ml/1 tablespoon olive oil
- 1 tablespoon water
- 1 tablespoon balsamic vinegar
- a little salt and freshly ground black pepper

Preparation:	15 minutes
Cooking:	50–60 minutes
Freezing:	no
Serves:	6

What you do:

Pre-heat the oven to 230°C/450°F/Gas 8. Cut each onion into four wedges. Cut the peppers, aubergine and courgettes into 1 inch chunks. Whisk the oil and water and rub this all over the vegetables with your hands so that all the vegetables are lightly coated. Place all the vegetables in a roasting tin, sprinkle with the garlic, a little salt and freshly ground black pepper. Bake in the oven for 50–60 minutes, turning occasionally until just tinged brown at the edges and soft in the middle. When cooked, remove the roasted vegetables from the oven, divide between 6 warm plates and sprinkle a little balsamic vinegar over each mound of vegetables.

Serve warm accompanied by the tzatziki (see page 44) in a separate bowl.

Per Serving	
Calories	56 kcal
Fat	2.9 g
Saturated Fat	0.44 g
Fibre	1.9 g

Garlic Toast with Tahina (Baba Ghanoush)

This delicious dish can be served as a light lunch in the garden to bring back memories of Mediterranean holidays. It's also very good as a starter and can be enjoyed regularly.

What you need:

- 8–10 slices crusty bread or ciabatta, sliced about 1 inch thick, lightly toasted on both sides
- 2 large cloves garlic
- 1 large aubergine
- 30–45 g/2–3 tablespoons tahina paste
- 75 ml/3 fl oz thick Greek yoghurt
- juice of 1 lemon
- pinch ground cumin (optional)
- 1 tablespoon parsley, chopped
- a few black olives or 1 tomato (sliced) as garnish
- a little salt

Preparation:	20 minutes
Cooking:	30–35 minutes
Freezing:	no
Serves:	4–5

What you do:

To make the aubergine pâté or 'caviare', pierce the aubergine in a few places with the point of a knife or a fork and cook under a hot grill, turning frequently, until the skin has blackened and the aubergine is soft. Or bake at 200°C/400°F/Gas 6 for about 30–45 minutes, depending on the size of the aubergine. Peel off the skin while still hot and mash the flesh to a purée, using a potato masher or fork. Beat in the lemon juice, tahina paste and 1 clove of garlic, peeled and well crushed. When cool, combine with the yoghurt and use to spread on toast or as a dip.

Cut the remaining clove of garlic in half and rub over one side of each piece of toast. Spread with aubergine pâté and garnish with chopped parsley and sliced olives or tomato. Serve warm.

Per Serving	(if serving 5)	(if serving 4)
Calories	261 kcal	327 kcal
Fat	9.2 g	12 g
Saturated Fat	2 g	2.6 g
Fibre	2.8 g	3.5 g

Salads & Dressings

Mixed Leaf Salad with Mint and Lemon Dressing

The yoghurt base for this dressing means it's low in fat — but very tasty. Try it with your favourite combination of fresh salad leaves.

What you need:

- 1 small head radicchio or half a head of frisée lettuce
- 1 head butterhead, lollo rossa or cos lettuce or half a head of iceberg lettuce
- 50 g/2 oz baby spinach leaves
- 50 g/2 oz rocket (optional)

For the Dressing:

- 6 tablespoons Greek style yoghurt
- 1 clove garlic, crushed
- 4 tablespoons chopped fresh mint
- 2 tablespoons lemon juice
- a little salt and freshly ground black pepper
- mint sprigs to garnish

Preparation:	10 minutes
Cooking:	none
Freezing:	no
Serves:	6–8

What you do:

First make the dressing. Beat the yoghurt, garlic, mint and lemon juice together in a shallow dish. Season and leave in the fridge until needed. Wash all the salad leaves under running cold water, drain, and dry thoroughly either with a dry tea towel or by spinning in a salad dryer. Tear all large leaves into bite-sized pieces. Arrange the leaves in a pyramid tower finishing off with a few sprigs of fresh mint. Serve the dressing separately. Serve with hot bruschetta (see page 28).

Note: Instead of spinach leaves and rocket, mustard leaves or other bitter leaves may be used. For variety in flavour, you may choose different herbs. Edible flowers, for example, nasturtium leaves and flowers add a peppery taste and extra colour. If using one predominant herb, this herb can also be substituted for the mint in the dressing to give a consistent flavour.

Per Serving	(if serving 8)	(if serving 6)
Calories	46 kcal	62 kcal
Fat	3.3 g	4.4 g
Saturated Fat	1.75 g	2.4 g
Fibre	0.7 g	0.9 g

Buffalo Mozzarella with Vine Tomatoes and Basil

Buffalo Mozzarella, while relatively high in fat, makes a delicious occasional starter — but keep to the small amounts used here and have plenty of vine or beef tomatoes. A drizzle of balsamic vinegar instead of basil dressing makes this dish lower in fat.

What you need:

- 150 g/5 oz pack buffalo mozzarella cheese, thinly sliced
- 24 leaves fresh basil
- 2–3 tablespoons basil and parsley dressing* or 1–2 tablespoons balsamic vinegar
- 450 g/1 lb vine tomatoes, thinly sliced
- a little salt and freshly ground black pepper

* see page 42

Preparation:	10 minutes
Cooking:	none
Freezing:	no
Serves:	4

What you do:

Arrange the slices of mozzarella and tomatoes in concentric circles on a serving platter. Season the tomatoes with a little salt and freshly ground black pepper. Scatter the basil leaves, torn into small pieces, over the tomatoes. Sprinkle the basil and parsley dressing or balsamic vinegar over the tomatoes. Serve with plenty of ciabatta bread warmed in the oven or with dough balls for an original touch (see page 111).

Per Serving
Calories	153 kcal
Fat	11 g
Saturated Fat	5.4 g
Fibre	1.5 g

Wild Mushroom Salad

This warm salad tastes delicious, especially if made with wild mushrooms which are rich in flavour. It also works well with large breakfast mushrooms on their own. Coat the salad leaves by tossing well in the warm dressing. This tip, which can be used for all salads, makes a small amount of dressing go further.

What you need:

- 175 g/6 oz wild mushrooms e.g. oyster/girroles/shitake
- 175 g/6 oz open cup mushrooms
- 1 clove garlic, peeled and chopped
- 15 ml/1 tablespoon olive oil
- mixed salad leaves to serve 4
- a few drops balsamic vinegar
- mixed herbs of your choice to garnish
- a little salt and freshly ground black pepper

Preparation:	5 minutes
Cooking:	5 minutes
Freezing:	no
Serves:	4

What you do:

Wipe the mushrooms clean with a damp cloth. Trim off the tips of the stalks. Slice the caps and stalks into even-sized pieces. In a heavy-based pan heat the oil. Add the garlic and cook for 1 minute; add the mushrooms and cook over a brisk heat for between 5 and 7 minutes. Remove from the heat, sprinkle with balsamic vinegar, season with a little salt and freshly ground black pepper and serve at once on a bed of mixed salad leaves. Coat well in the warm dressing. Garnish with herbs such as parsley, chervil and mint.

Per Serving	
Calories	50 kcal
Fat	4 g
Saturated Fat	2 g
Fibre	2 g

Roasted Pepper Salad with Spicy Dressing

Another variation on the delicious roasted peppers theme, this time given an oriental twist and a little heat with chillies. This no-fat dressing can be used to spice up any salad.

What you need:
- 4 sweet peppers, red, yellow, green and orange

For the Dressing:
- 1 small red chilli, deseeded and very finely chopped
- 15 g/½ oz fresh root ginger, peeled and grated, or very finely chopped
- 1 bunch thin scallions, trimmed and very finely chopped
- 4 tablespoons light soy sauce
- 4 tablespoons fresh lemon juice
- 1 tablespoon white wine or cider vinegar
- 2 tablespoons clear honey

Preparation:	10 minutes
Cooking:	20 minutes
Freezing:	no
Serves:	4 (dressing makes sufficient quantity for 10–12)

What you do:
Cut the peppers in half and carefully remove seeds and any white pith. Place peppers, cut side down, on a baking sheet. Roast peppers at 220°C/425°F/Gas 7 for 15–20 minutes until the skin is loosened and beginning to blister and blacken. Set aside to cool slightly (alternatively grill, turning frequently, so that they cook evenly). Try not to let the blisters burst or the skin is difficult to remove. When cool enough to handle, remove the skin and cut into thick slices and place in a serving dish.

Meanwhile, combine all the dressing ingredients in a bowl and mix well. To serve, spoon the dressing over the peppers.

Note: The recipe for the dressing gives 8–12 servings. However, it's good with a variety of grilled foods such as fish, meat and poultry and will keep for a few days in a clean, covered jar in the fridge.

Per Serving	
Calories	102 kcal
Fat	0.7 g
Saturated Fat	0.1 g
Fibre	2.8 g

Sunshine Tomato Salad with Toasted Heart Croutons

Brighten up your day with this sunshine tomato salad! Toasted heart croutons make this salad look as good as it tastes. Try toasting croutons instead of frying them and add to your favourite salads and soups.

What you need:

- ½ head iceberg lettuce
- 50 g/2 oz rocket
- 50 g/2oz lamb's lettuce
- 25 g/1 oz beansprouts
- 100 g/4 oz cherry tomatoes, halved
- 1–2 yellow peppers, deseeded and sliced into strips
- 50 g/2 oz baby spinach leaves (optional)
- 4 thin slices brown bread

For the Dressing:

- 30 ml/2 tablespoons olive oil
- 15 ml/1 dessertspoon balsamic vinegar
- pinch of sugar
- 1 small clove garlic, peeled, crushed and finely chopped
- a little salt and freshly ground black pepper

Preparation:	15–20 minutes
Cooking:	none
Freezing:	no
Serves:	4

What you do:

Tear the iceberg lettuce into bite-size pieces. Wash all the salad leaves in cold water. Drain and pat dry. Put the salad leaves into a bowl and add the peppers and tomatoes. For the dressing, place all the ingredients into a screw-top jar and shake vigorously to combine.

Pre-heat the grill. Using a small heart-shaped cutter, stamp out shapes from the bread and grill until golden on both sides. To serve, pour the dressing on the salad and toss lightly. Scatter the warm croutons on the salad and serve at once.

Per Serving	
Calories	154 kcal
Fat	8.5 g
Saturated Fat	1.2 g
Fibre	2.8 g

Basil and Parsley Dressing

This herby dressing is lower in fat than traditional pesto, yet gives plenty of flavour to pasta. You can also spread it on French bread slices and grill for a delicious snack.

What you need:

- 2 handfuls basil, very finely chopped
- 2 handfuls parsley, very finely chopped
- 1 clove garlic, peeled, crushed and very finely chopped
- ½ dried chilli (optional)
- 3 tablespoons olive oil
- a little salt and freshly ground black pepper

Preparation:	10 minutes
Cooking:	none
Freezing:	no
Serves:	2–4

What you do:

Place the herbs and garlic in a bowl. Add the oil and toss until all the herbs are lightly coated with oil. Season with a little salt and freshly ground black pepper.

Note: It's important that the herbs be absolutely fresh and used in quantity. This dressing can be used in the tomato and mozzarella salad (see page 38). It may also be used as a herby addition to a green salad or to a home-made tomato sauce for pasta. It can be added on its own to cooked pasta and topped with a little grated parmesan.

Per Serving	(if serving 4)	(if serving 2)
Calories	102 kcal	203 kcal
Fat	11.3 g	23 g
Saturated Fat	1.6 g	3.2 g
Fibre	0.05 g	0.1 g

Lime and Coriander Yoghurt Dressing

Yoghurt makes the ideal base for a low-fat dressing. Lime, coriander and ginger give this dressing an oriental/Eastern flavour. Also delicious with Mexican food instead of higher-fat sour cream.

What you need:

- 1 cm/½ inch piece fresh root ginger, peeled and grated
- 1 clove garlic, crushed
- 150 ml/¼ pint low-fat bio yoghurt
- rind of 1 lime, finely grated
- 30 ml/2 tablespoons fresh coriander, chopped
- squeeze of lime juice
- coriander sprigs to garnish

Preparation:	5 minutes
Cooking:	none
Freezing:	no
Serves:	4

What you do:

In a bowl mix the yoghurt with the ginger, garlic, lime rind, coriander and lime juice to taste.

Chill until ready to serve. Garnish before serving with coriander sprigs.

Per Serving	
Calories	23 kcal
Fat	0.3 g
Saturated Fat	0.19 g
Fibre	0.04 g

Tzatziki

This delicious yoghurt and garlic dip from Greece is low in fat and can be used with raw vegetables, toasted pitta bread fingers or roasted vegetables. It tastes so good you can even use it on bread instead of a spread, with cold meats or cheese for a tasty lunch.

What you need:

- ½ cucumber, washed
- 200 ml/7 fl oz carton thick Greek yoghurt
- ½ teaspoon white wine vinegar
- 1 teaspoon olive oil
- 1 teaspoon fresh mint, chopped
- 1 clove garlic, crushed and chopped
- a little salt and freshly ground black pepper to taste

Preparation:	15–20 minutes
Cooking:	none
Freezing:	no
Serves:	4

What you do:

Cut the cucumber into julienne strips or grate very coarsely into a sieve. Set aside to drain for 10 minutes, then pat dry with kitchen paper. Combine all the other ingredients. Just before serving, fold in the cucumber. Use as a dip with crudités, or serve as an accompaniment to curries and spicy foods.

Note: In winter use frozen mint, or half a teaspoonful of dried mint plus one teaspoonful of chopped fresh parsley. Double quantities with julienned or diced cucumber makes a pleasant side salad for 4 people.

Per Serving	
Calories	87 kcal
Fat	7 g
Saturated Fat	3.25 g
Fibre	0.2 g

Spicy Red Pepper Salsa

This spicy red pepper salsa can be served as a dressing with barbecued food, hamburgers, gammon steaks or chops, with lots of salad and crusty bread. Or serve as a starter with freshly prepared raw vegetables such as celery sticks, carrot sticks, tomato wedges, cucumber chunks or thinly cut fingers of pitta bread.

What you need:

- 1 red pepper, deseeded and chopped
- 1 clove garlic, crushed
- 2 large ripe plum tomatoes/½ tin plum tomatoes, drained well
- 1 small onion, chopped
- juice of ½ lemon
- 1 fresh red chilli, deseeded and chopped
- 15 ml/1 tablespoon olive oil
- 2 tablespoons parsley
- a little salt and freshly ground black pepper

Preparation:	10 minutes
Cooking:	none
Freezing:	no
Serves:	4

What you do:

Place all the ingredients in a food processor and blend evenly but not too finely.

Keep in the fridge until ready to use.

Per Serving	
Calories	62 kcal
Fat	4 g
Saturated Fat	0.6 g
Fibre	1.3 g

Fish

Steamed Salmon with Mustard and Chive Dressing

Salmon, always a popular choice, is also a heart-healthy food being rich in polyunsaturated fats that may help protect against heart disease. This mustard and chive dressing also tastes good with chicken.

What you need:
- 4 salmon fillets (about 175–225 g/6–8 oz each in weight)
- a little oil to grease the greaseproof paper

Preparation:	15 minutes
Cooking:	6–8 minutes
Freezing:	no
Serves:	4

For the Dressing:
- 2 teaspoons wholegrain mustard
- ½ tablespoon white wine vinegar
- 30 ml/2 tablespoons olive oil
- 1–2 teaspoons fresh chives, finely snipped
- a little salt and freshly ground black pepper

What you do:
Wrap the salmon fillets in individual pieces of lightly oiled (use a brush) seasoned greaseproof paper and put in a large steamer with water boiling rapidly. Cover with a tight-fitting lid and steam for 6–8 minutes. The salmon should look opaque when you unwrap it. Meanwhile, in a liquidiser whisk together the mustard and the vinegar. Pour the oil into the mustard mixture in a steady stream, whisking vigorously as you do so. Season with a little salt and pepper. Serve the salmon fillets on heated plates and, just before serving, add the chives to the dressing and spoon the dressing over the salmon fillets. Serve with baked potatoes and a green vegetable or green salad.

Per Serving	
Calories	432 kcal
Fat	30 g
Saturated Fat	5 g
Fibre	0.2 g

Cod Steak with Spicy Thai Sauce

This spicy Thai sauce gives a sharp taste to the cod steaks. Make it the day before and you'll have a meal in minutes the following day. Try to eat fish at least twice a week, choosing oily fish regularly.

What you need:
- 4 x 150–175 g/5–6 oz cod steaks
- 5 ml/1 teaspoon olive oil
- a little salt and freshly ground black pepper

Preparation:	15 minutes
Cooking:	10–15 minutes
Freezing:	no
Serves:	4

For the Thai Sauce:
- 1 bunch or packet coriander
- 2 cm/1 inch piece fresh root ginger, peeled and sliced
- 2 green chillies, deseeded and chopped
- 100 ml/3½ fl oz light mayonnaise
- squeeze of fresh lemon
- dash of fish sauce or soy sauce
- 2 garlic cloves, halved

What you do:
Make the sauce by blanching the coriander in boiling water for 1 minute, drain and refresh with cold water. Squeeze out the excess water. Whisk in a food processor with the rest of the sauce ingredients. Chill in the refrigerator, preferably overnight, or at least for 1–2 hours. Season the cod steaks with a little salt and black pepper and place on a baking tray lightly greased by brushing with one teaspoon of olive oil and cook for 15–20 minutes at 190°C/375°F/Gas 5. Alternatively, season the fish, brush with olive oil and cook under a hot grill for 3–5 minutes on each side. To serve, place the fish on a bed of rice or herbed potato mash (made with mashed potato, a handful of any chopped herb of your choice and 5 ml/1 teaspoon olive oil) and serve the Thai sauce on the side together with a tomato salad.

Per Serving
Calories	226 kcal
Fat	9.5 g
Saturated Fat	0.4 g
Fibre	0.03 g

◀ Easy Home-made Brown Bread (page 108)

▼ Winter Fruit Compote (page 98)

◀ A selection of Home-made Muffins (pages 115, 116, 117)

Focaccia Pizza (page 75) ▶

Seared Tuna with Mexican Salsa

Fresh tuna is a special treat and is good for your heart! Try it with a marinade and salsa combination for a Mexican delight!

What you need:
- 4 x 150–175 g/5–6 oz tuna steaks

For the Marinade:
- 15 ml/1 tablespoon olive oil
- 1 clove garlic, peeled and crushed
- ¼ teaspoon ground cumin
- ¼ teaspoon ground coriander
- juice of ½ a lime
- a little salt and freshly ground black pepper

For the Salsa:
- 1 clove garlic, peeled, crushed and chopped
- juice of 1½ limes
- ¼ teaspoon ground cumin
- ¼ teaspoon ground coriander
- 2 tablespoons fresh coriander, de-stalked and finely chopped
- 1 small red onion, very finely chopped
- 1 firm, ripe avocado, peeled, stoned and chopped
- 225 g/8 oz firm, ripe tomatoes, peeled, deseeded and chopped
- pinch of sugar
- ½ mild red chilli, deseeded and very finely chopped (optional)
- a little salt and freshly ground black pepper

Preparation:	30 minutes
Cooking:	7 minutes
Freezing:	no
Serves:	4

What you do:
Combine all the marinade ingredients: the olive oil, garlic, cumin, coriander, lime, and season. Pour into a wide dish and rub this on both sides of the tuna steaks. Chill for about half an hour to allow the flavour to develop.

In a deep bowl combine all the salsa ingredients: the garlic, lime juice, ground cumin, ground coriander, fresh coriander, onion, avocado, tomatoes, sugar and mild red chilli.

Pre-heat a griddle or flat pan until really hot. Take tuna from the marinade and shake off any excess marinade. Place in the pan and sear for 2–3 minutes on each side. Tuna can be tough and dry if overcooked, so watch it carefully and take off the heat when it's still slightly translucent in the centre. Serve at once, garnished with sprigs of coriander, with the salsa and a green salad.

Note: The chilli is a matter of taste — if it is too fiery, it will overwhelm the taste of the tuna.

Per Serving
Calories   394 kcal
Fat   20 g
Saturated Fat   4.5 g
Fibre   2 g

Salmon with Lime, Ginger and Coriander Parcels

These salmon parcels keep all the flavour of the fish. Salmon, an oily fish, is rich in Omega-3 fats, which may help protect against heart disease.

What you need:

- 2 salmon fillets
  (about 150–175 g/5–6 oz each)
- 1 teaspoon grated fresh ginger
- grated zest and juice of 1 lime
- 1 clove garlic, crushed
- 1 tablespoon fresh coriander, chopped
- a little salt and freshly ground black pepper
- chopped coriander or parsley to garnish

Preparation:	10 minutes
Cooking:	25 minutes
Freezing:	no
Serves:	2

What you do:

In a small bowl mix the ginger, lime zest and half the juice, garlic and coriander. Next, take two pieces of tin foil about 9 inches square, place a salmon fillet on each, season, and spoon over the seasoning mixture. Fold the long sides of the tin foil inwards and then fold the remaining sides in, making a small parcel. Place the parcels on a baking sheet and bake in a pre-heated oven at 200°C/400°F/Gas 6 for about 20–25 minutes (the exact time depends on the thickness of the fillets). Serve garnished with chopped coriander or parsley and a wedge of lime. Wild rice, mixed with white rice, and a tomato salad make good accompaniments.

Per Serving	
Calories	321 kcal
Fat	18 g
Saturated Fat	1.7 g
Fibre	0.3 g

Hake with Rosemary and Garlic

Rosemary and garlic — always a tasty combination — give a good flavour to the hake in this quick and easy meal. Any firm white fish can be used if hake isn't easily available.

What you need:

- 700g/1½ lb hake, filleted, with skin on
- 2 cloves garlic, cut into fine slices
- a few sprigs of fresh rosemary
- 8 ml/½ tablespoon pure vegetable oil
- a little salt and freshly ground black pepper

Preparation:	3 minutes
Cooking:	14 minutes
Freezing:	no
Serves:	4

What you do:

Cut the fish into four pieces. With the tip of a small, sharp knife make small holes in between the flakes of the fish and slip a slice of garlic and a leaf of rosemary into each. Heat oil in a pan until very hot. Place fish fillets in the pan, skin side down, and sear for 2 minutes. If the pan is oven-proof, place it in the oven; if not, use a fish slice to place the fish on a well-heated baking sheet. Cook at 190°C/375°F/Gas 5 for 12 minutes. Serve hot with a green vegetable and new potatoes.

Per Serving
Calories	180 kcal
Fat	5.9 g
Saturated Fat	0.7 g
Fibre	0.03 g

Meat

Baked Spicy Spare Ribs

These spare ribs can be barbecued and enjoyed outdoors in summer or oven baked in colder weather. Try to get lean meaty spare ribs.

What you need:
- 1.8 kg/4 lb lean meaty pork spare ribs (approx. 2 sheets of ribs)

For the Sauce:
- 3–4 large cloves garlic, crushed, peeled and finely chopped
- 1–2 small fresh chillies, deseeded and finely chopped, or 2 tablespoons hot chilli sauce (both, if you like things very hot)
- 150 ml/¼ pint canned tomatoes, liquidised with juice
- 75 ml/3 fl oz cider vinegar
- 5 tablespoons honey
- 2 tablespoons Dijon mustard
- dash of Worcestershire sauce
- 300 ml/11 fl oz chicken stock
- 15 ml/1 tablespoon pure vegetable oil
- a little salt and freshly ground black pepper

Preparation:	15 minutes
Cooking:	1 hour 40 minutes
Freezing:	no
Serves:	6

What you do:
Pre-heat oven to 190°C/375°F/Gas 5. To make the sauce, heat the oil in a saucepan over a moderate heat. Add the garlic and fresh chillies (if using) and stir for about 30 seconds. Add the tomatoes, vinegar, honey, mustard, Worcestershire sauce, chilli sauce (if using), stock and seasoning. Bring to the boil over a high heat and simmer for about 15 minutes.

Cut each sheet of ribs into two even pieces and arrange on a wire tray in a large roasting tin. Brush with some of the sauce. Roast for 30 minutes. Excess fat will drain off into the roasting tin. Brush the ribs with more sauce and roast for a further hour, turning and brushing with more sauce occasionally.

Per Serving
Calories	500 kcal
Fat	22 g
Saturated Fat	7 g
Fibre	0.3 g

Pork with Mango Salsa

This is a really simple, tasty dish and has been a regular favourite of restaurants participating in the annual Happy Heart Eat Out restaurant campaign.

What you need:
- 1 x 350 g/12 oz pork fillet, well trimmed

For the Marinade:
- 15 ml/1 tablespoon hot chilli sauce
- 15 ml/1 tablespoon vegetable oil
- 15 ml/1 tablespoon dry sherry
- 15 ml/1 tablespoon light soy sauce

For the Salsa:
- 1 red pepper, deseeded and chopped into small dice
- 1 ripe mango, skinned and diced
- 3–4 scallions, finely chopped
- 1 tablespoon hot chilli sauce
- a little salt and freshly ground black pepper

Preparation:	25 minutes *plus* 30–40 minutes marinade
Cooking:	16–20 minutes
Freezing:	no
Serves:	3

What you do:
Spread the marinade mixture over the pork and leave for as long as possible, at least 30–40 minutes. Combine the salsa ingredients and leave in the fridge until ready to serve.

Under a moderate grill or on a barbecue, cook the pork for 8–10 minutes on each side. Carve the meat into thin slices and serve with the salsa.

Suggested accompaniments for this dish are new baby potatoes and French beans or mange-tout.

Note: Instead of using mango you can make a delicious red pepper salsa (see page 45).

Per Serving	
Calories	287 kcal
Fat	13 g
Saturated Fat	3 g
Fibre	2.5 g

Mediterranean Beef
and Vegetables

This delicious steak recipe for a special meal will transport you back to a Mediterranean seaside village! You can add a baked potato if you like, but crusty bread is really all you need.

What you need:

- 4 small sirloin steaks (about 100 g/4 oz each) 1 inch thick, trimmed of excess fat
- 15 ml/1 tablespoon olive oil
- 4 cloves garlic, peeled and crushed
- 3 tablespoons sundried tomato paste
- 150 ml/¼ pint red wine
- 3 tablespoons fresh oregano, chopped
- 1 small aubergine, cut into 2 inch slices (optional)
- 2 small courgettes, cut lengthways into two pieces
- 1 yellow pepper, halved, deseeded and cut into 8 pieces
- 1 red pepper, halved, deseeded and cut into 8 pieces
- a little salt and freshly ground black pepper

Preparation:	15 minutes *plus* 1½ hours in marinade
Cooking:	35 minutes
Freezing:	no
Serves:	4

What you do:

Place the steaks in a shallow dish. Mix together the olive oil, garlic, sundried tomato paste, red wine, oregano and seasoning. Pour marinade over the steaks and turn to coat on both sides. Cover and marinade in the fridge for one hour or more. Thirty minutes before you begin cooking, add the prepared vegetables to the marinade. Replace in the fridge.

Place all the vegetables on the grill rack. It is important to keep the heat of the grill low or the outsides will burn before the vegetables are tender. Grill for about 25 minutes, or until tender and brown, turning at least two or three times and basting occasionally with the marinade. Remove and keep warm while you cook the steaks. Turn the grill up to high and grill the steaks, turning once, until the meat is done. This will take between 7–10 minutes. Meanwhile, pour remaining marinade into a small saucepan and heat until it reaches boiling point and cook until reduced a little. Place steaks and vegetables on hot plates, drizzle the reduced marinade over each serving. Serve with crusty bread to soak up the juices.

Per Serving	
Calories	261 kcal
Fat	7.5 g
Saturated Fat	2.3 g
Fibre	3.6 g

Low-fat Lasagne

This is a variation on classic lasagne which uses low-fat ingredients and cooking methods to provide a healthier alternative without loosing any of the flavour. Be less generous with the Parmesan, or use low-fat cheese instead.

What you need:

For the Meat Sauce:

- 450 g/1 lb lean minced beef
- 1 large onion, finely chopped
- 5 large cloves garlic, finely chopped
- 1 stick celery, finely chopped
- 1 large carrot, finely chopped
- 375 ml/13 fl oz beef/chicken stock
- 400 g/2 x 14 oz cans chopped tomatoes
- 1 teaspoon dried oregano/mixed herbs
- 1 bay leaf
- ½ teaspoon dried nutmeg
- 1 tablespoon tomato purée
- 100 ml/4 fl oz water
- a little salt and freshly ground black pepper

For the Low-fat White Sauce:

- 600 ml/1 pint low-fat milk
- 1 small onion, peeled and studded with 3 whole cloves
- 1 bay leaf
- 2 tablespoons cornflour
- 3 tablespoons cold low-fat milk
- 1 teaspoon mustard of your choice

- a little grated Parmesan/low-fat cheese
- 9–12 lasagne sheets

Preparation:	¾ hour
Cooking:	1¼ hours
Freezing:	no
Serves:	4–6

What you do:

To make the meat sauce, heat a heavy-based casserole over a moderate heat, add the minced beef and break it down with a wooden spoon. Keep moving the mince around until the meat is lightly browned. Drain off all excess fat, then add the chopped onion, garlic, celery, carrot and cook gently stirring until the vegetables are softening. Add the stock and bring to the boil. Cook, stirring for a couple of minutes. Add the chopped tomato, oregano, bay leaf, nutmeg, tomato purée and water. Season and stir well, then simmer very gently for about an hour until a thick sauce is produced, stirring occasionally and adding a little water if the mixture seems to be drying out.

To make the low-fat white sauce: in a saucepan, rinsed with cold water, gently heat the milk, the clove studded onion and the bay leaf. Slowly bring to the boil, then remove from the heat and leave for 15 minutes. Strain.

Blend together the cornflour and 3 tablespoons of cold milk, then gradually add the remaining milk mixture. Return to the rinsed pan and cook over a moderate heat, stirring all the time to make a smooth sauce. Simmer over a low heat for 1 minute. Add mustard and extra milk if necessary.

To assemble and cook the lasagne, pre-heat a moderate oven 180°C/350°F/Gas 4. Lightly oil a large shallow ovenproof dish. Spread a thin layer of the meat sauce over the dish. Arrange a single layer of pasta sheets over the sauce. Top this with another layer of meat, then a layer of low-fat white sauce and a light sprinkling of low-fat cheese. Repeat layers as before, finishing with a layer of pasta, reserving some of the low-fat white sauce to top the pasta. Sprinkle lightly with cheese and cook in the pre-heated oven for about 45 minutes until bubbling and golden brown. Serve with a crisp green salad with low-fat dressing and garlic bread (see page 107).

Recipe by Georgina Campbell. Taken from *Go for Low Fat Healthy Eating* magazine, 1999, Health Promotion Unit.

Per Serving	
Calories	336 kcal
Fat	11 g
Saturated Fat	5 g
Fibre	2.4 g

Spicy Hamburgers with Guacamole

Home-made hamburgers are more economical, healthier and tastier. Add your favourite herbs for a different flavour. Top with a spoonful or two of guacamole for a taste of Mexico. The guacamole also makes a delicious starter served with raw vegetables or pitta bread fingers.

What you need:
- 450–700 g/1–1½ lb round steak, trimmed and coarsely chopped
- 2 cloves garlic
- 1 tablespoon Dijon mustard
- handful of coriander leaves, chopped
- a little salt and freshly ground black pepper

For the Guacamole:
- 1 ripe avocado
- 1 small clove garlic, crushed
- 1 tablespoon lime juice
- 1 tomato peeled, deseeded and chopped
- ¼ teaspoon chilli powder
- ¼ teaspoon each of salt and freshly ground black pepper

Preparation:	20 minutes
Cooking:	8–10 minutes
Freezing:	yes (as raw hamburgers)
Serves:	4

What you do:
Place the steak, garlic, mustard, coriander and the seasoning in a food processor. Blend until combined; do not over-process. Shape the meat into 8 burgers. Set aside. To make the guacamole, cut the avocado in half and scoop out the flesh. Mash the flesh with a fork. Add the garlic, lime juice, tomato, chilli powder and seasoning. Mix well. Cook the hamburgers under a hot grill for about 4–5 minutes on each side or until cooked through. Place 2 hamburgers on each plate and top with a generous dollop of guacamole and scatter fresh coriander on top. Serve with baked potato and a tomato and onion salad.

Per Serving	
Calories	478 kcal
Fat	19 g
Saturated Fat	5.4 g
Fibre	1 g

Poultry

Chicken and Garlic Parmesan

Another Happy Heart Eat Out recipe — this chicken dish, soaked in milk, keeps the chicken fillets succulent and moist. Remember, Parmesan is quite high in fat — so do weigh out two ounces.

What you need:

- 4 boneless chicken breast fillets
- 4 large cloves garlic
- 225 ml/8 fl oz milk
- 2 heaped tablespoons fresh parsley, finely chopped
- 50 g/2 oz Parmesan cheese, grated
- a little olive oil
- a little salt and freshly ground black pepper

Preparation:	20 minutes *plus* 4 hours marinade
Cooking:	30 minutes
Freezing:	no
Serves:	4

What you do:

Arrange the chicken fillets in a shallow dish. Crush the garlic cloves and add this to the milk. Season with a little salt and pepper and pour over the chicken breasts. Cover the dish with clingfilm and leave in a cool place or the fridge for at least 4 hours or overnight, turning the chicken breasts at least once.

Pre-heat the oven to 220°C/425°F/Gas 7 and put in a shallow greased ovenproof dish. Combine the Parmesan, parsley and a little seasoning together on a plate. Spread out some absorbent kitchen paper on a flat surface.

Remove the chicken from the fridge. Take one piece at a time and carefully place on the kitchen paper to absorb the milk (take care not to disturb the garlic). Put the chicken fillets into the dish and brush them with a little oil. Cover with the Parmesan cheese mixture and bake for about 30 minutes until golden brown. If necessary, reduce the heat halfway through the cooking. Serve immediately with green summer vegetables or a crisp green salad and a baked potato.

Per Serving	
Calories	192 kcal
Fat	6 g
Saturated Fat	3.4 g
Fibre	0.2 g

Chicken Fajitas

A delicious Mexican meal that's quick and easy to make, very tasty and low in fat —
a regular favourite to enjoy casually with a few friends.

What you need:

- 450 g/1 lb chicken breast, thinly sliced
- 15 ml/1 tablespoon pure vegetable oil
- 1 lime, halved
- 1 packet fajita seasoning mix
- 1 green pepper, deseeded and sliced
- 1 red pepper, deseeded and sliced
- 1 medium onion, sliced
- 12 flour tortilla pancakes
- 125 g/4½ oz low-fat fromage frais

Preparation:	20 minutes
Cooking:	10 minutes
Freezing:	no
Serves:	6

What you do:

Heat the oil in a wok. Add the chicken and stir-fry for about 4 minutes. Sprinkle with fajita seasoning mix, stir-fry for 1 minute. Add lime juice and mix in. Add the peppers and onion and cook for a further 3–6 minutes until tender, splashing in a little water if necessary, making sure not to overcook the vegetables. Heat the flour tortillas according to instructions on the packet. Fill each tortilla with the fajita mixture, 1 tablespoon of salsa and 1 dessertspoon of fromage frais. Roll up tortillas and serve with a green salad.

Note: For salsa see page 45.

Per Serving
Calories	427 kcal
Fat	6.3 g
Saturated Fat	1 g
Fibre	4 g

Thai Green Chicken Curry

Thai food is growing in popularity and it's easy to see why in this spicy, coconut-flavoured curry. For a special treat, stir in prawn tails a few minutes before the end of cooking — until just warmed through.

What you need:

- 4 chicken fillets
- 15 ml/1 tablespoon pure vegetable oil
- 1–2 tablespoons green Thai curry paste
- 200 g/7 oz broccoli florets
- 300 ml/10 fl oz coconut milk*
- 1 small red chilli, deseeded and chopped
- a good handful fresh coriander

Preparation:	15 minutes
Cooking:	20–25 minutes
Freezing:	no
Serves:	4

What you do:

Cut chicken into small pieces and brown in the hot oil in a wok. Lift out and stir the curry paste into the juices in the pan. Cook, stirring, for 1 minute, then return the chicken to the wok or pan. Mix until well coated with the paste. Stir in the coconut milk, cover and simmer gently for 10 minutes. Blanch the broccoli in boiling water for 2 minutes, drain and add to the chicken. Cook for 2–3 minutes more, stirring occasionally, until the sauce has thickened and the chicken is completely tender. Stir in the chopped coriander, saving some as a garnish. Serve in bowls with freshly cooked Thai or long-grain rice.

*Note: To make coconut milk, melt 2 sachets of creamed coconut or 50 g/½ oz grated block coconut in 300 ml/½ pint boiling water.

Per Serving, when made with 2 sachets creamed coconut

Calories	337 kcal
Fat	26 g
Saturated Fat	15 g
Fibre	4.8 g

Per Serving, when made with 50 g grated block coconut

Calories	265 kcal
Fat	17 g
Saturated Fat	9.1 g
Fibre	1.3 g

Chinese Turkey Kebabs with Noodles and Beansprouts

Turkey, naturally low in fat, tastes really good with this Chinese sauce. Noodles are a good starch alternative to rice or pasta. The low calorie value also makes this a good choice for slimmers.

What you need:

- 450 g/1 lb turkey fillets, cut in strips
- 3 tablespoons dark soy sauce
- 1 tablespoon tomato purée
- 2 teaspoons sugar
- 150 ml/¼ pint hot chicken or vegetable stock
- 275 g/10 oz egg noodles
- 100 g/4 oz beansprouts

Preparation:	10 minutes
Cooking:	10 minutes
Freezing:	no
Serves:	4

What you do:

In a bowl mix together the soy sauce, tomato purée and sugar. Then pour half into a saucepan with the stock. Add the turkey strips to the remaining sauce in the bowl and stir to coat well. Thread the turkey strips on to 8 skewers, making a zigzag turkey pattern. Grill or barbecue for about 6–8 minutes, turning every now and then, until evenly and thoroughly cooked. Meanwhile, put the noodles into a large saucepan, cover with boiling water, bring to the boil and simmer as directed on the packet. Bring the tomato sauce and stock to the boil, add the beansprouts and gently simmer for a few minutes. Drain the noodles, then add to the sauce and toss well. Divide between warmed plates (2 kebabs on each). Serve immediately with a tomato or other salad of your choice.

Note: This Chinese sauce can also be used on other meats and white fish.

Per Serving	
Calories	422 kcal
Fat	7.9 g
Saturated Fat	2.17 g
Fibre	2.6 g

Vegetarian

Halloumi Cheese Kebabs
with Lime and Coriander Dip

For a delicious vegetarian meal that even non-vegetarians will want to taste and enjoy, try these Halloumi cheese kebabs. It is worth spending extra time finding out where you can get Halloumi cheese!

What you need:

- 350 g/12 oz Halloumi cheese
- juice and zest of 1 lime
- 1 clove garlic, finely chopped
- 1 heaped tablespoon fresh coriander leaves, very finely chopped
- 135 g/3 tablespoons Greek yoghurt or bio natural yoghurt
- 5 ml/1 teaspoon olive oil
- a little salt and freshly ground black pepper

Preparation:	20 minutes
Cooking:	5–10 minutes
Freezing:	no
Serves:	4

What you do:

Mix all the ingredients except the cheese and oil in a small bowl. Cover and leave in the fridge to blend the flavours.

Unwrap the cheese and pat it dry with kitchen paper. Using a sharp knife, slice it into squares. Thread the squares on to kebab sticks. Brush very lightly with oil and barbecue or grill until golden brown. When the kebabs are ready, serve straightaway on a warm plate with the dressing served separately in a ramekin dish. This is good served with a green salad tossed with a handful of pine nuts and some new potatoes.

Note: Halloumi cheese can be obtained in delicatessens specialising in exotic foods and in some larger supermarkets at the cheese counter.

Per Serving	
Calories	348 kcal
Fat	27 g
Saturated Fat	15 g
Fibre	0.2 g

Cheese, Leek and Potato Gratin

Garlic and crème fraîche make a delicious creamy topping for this tasty potato gratin. Cheese, rich in protein, makes this a healthy vegetarian dish. Remember, cheese (preferably low-fat), eggs and nuts must be added to vegetarian meals to provide adequate protein. Mature cheddar cheese is used in the dish for extra flavour — so you need less.

What you need:
- 700 g/1½ lb new potatoes, thickly sliced
- 2 leeks, thinly sliced
- 2 cloves garlic
- 200 ml/7 fl oz carton low-fat crème fraîche
- 75 g/3 oz mature cheddar
- a little salt and freshly ground black pepper

Preparation:	20 minutes
Cooking:	about 20 minutes
Freezing:	no
Serves:	4

What you do:
Pre-heat the grill. Add the potatoes to a pan of boiling water and cook for 7–10 minutes or until tender. Add the leeks for the last remaining 3 minutes of cooking. Meanwhile, crush the garlic cloves and stir into the crème fraîche. Drain the potatoes and leeks and season. Put the potato mixture into a baking dish. Spread spoonfuls of garlic crème fraîche over the potatoes, then grate the cheese on top. Grill for 3–4 minutes until the crème fraîche has melted into the potatoes and the cheese is golden and bubbling. Serve immediately with broccoli or french beans.

Note: For non-vegetarians, chopped left-over cooked chicken or boiled ham can be added to the potato and leek mixture before putting it into the baking dish. Make sure meats are well heated through before adding.

Per Serving
Calories   416 kcal
Fat   25 g
Saturated Fat   16 g
Fibre   2.7 g

Mango and Chilli Quesadillas

A quesadilla (pronounced kay-sa-dee-a) is a turnover made with a Mexican tortilla and usually filled with cheese. Other optional fillings for non-vegetarians may include ham, cooked chicken, green chillies or re-fried beans. Top with salsa for a delicious lunch or light supper.

What you need:

- 4 soft 8 inch/20 cm flour tortillas
- 100 g/4 oz mature cheddar cheese, grated
- 1 mango, peeled, stoned and finely sliced
- 1–2 green chillies, peeled and finely chopped
- 4 tablespoons spring onion, chopped
- 10 ml/2 teaspoons pure vegetable oil
- salsa (see page 45)
- shredded lettuce

Preparation:	20 minutes
Cooking:	16–20 minutes
Freezing:	no
Serves:	4

What you do:

Sprinkle half of each tortilla with cheese, mango slices, chillies and onions. Moisten the edges of the tortillas and press firmly together. Brush a non-stick frying pan with 1 teaspoon/5 ml of oil. Heat over a medium high heat. Cook two of the tortillas on the pan for about 4 minutes on each side until golden or the cheese melts. Remove from the heat, cut into 3 wedges, and repeat with the remaining tortillas. To serve, top with salsa and shredded lettuce.

Alternative cooking methods: brush the folded tortillas lightly with oil, place on a baking tray and cook in the oven at 200°C/400°F/Gas 6 for 15–20 minutes until crisp on top and heated through; or spray the folded tortillas with low-fat cooking spray and cook under a hot grill.

Per Serving	
Calories	268 kcal
Fat	8.5 g
Saturated Fat	3.5 g
Fibre	2.7 g

Cherry Tomato and Basil Omelette

An omelette with a difference. You'll love it! The combination of eggs, milk and some Parmesan cheese means you get your required protein.

What you need:

- 450 g/1 lb small cherry tomatoes
- 4 eggs
- 1 clove garlic, chopped
- 25 g/1 oz plain flour
- 200 ml/7 fl oz carton low-fat crème fraîche
- 4 tablespoons low-fat milk
- handful fresh basil, chopped
- 50 g/2 oz Parmesan, grated
- a little oil for greasing
- a little salt and freshly ground black pepper

Preparation:	10 minutes
Cooking:	20–25 minutes
Freezing:	no
Serves:	4

What you do:

Pre-heat the oven to 190°C/375°F/Gas 5. Lightly grease a large round baking dish or quiche dish (23 cm/9 inch dish about 4 cm/½ inch deep). Spread the tomatoes over the base and scatter the garlic on top. Bake the tomatoes and garlic for 5–10 minutes to heat the tomatoes thoroughly. Beat the eggs in a large bowl, then beat in the flour using a wire whisk. Beat in the crème fraîche and the milk until the batter is smooth. Stir in the basil and the Parmesan cheese keeping 1 tablespoon of each for the topping. Season with a little salt and black pepper. Pour this mixture over the tomatoes and sprinkle with the remaining cheese, basil and a little black pepper. Bake for 20 minutes until puffed up and golden on top. Serve warm with green salad and crusty bread.

Per Serving	
Calories	289 kcal
Fat	21 g
Saturated Fat	11 g
Fibre	1.3 g

Focaccia Pizza

A delicious pizza can be made using plain focaccia bread as a base. It's also quick and easy — real Friday evening food!

What you need:
- 1 plain focaccia (see page 109) or buy in large supermarkets/delicatessens

For the Tomato Sauce:
- 400 g/14 oz tin chopped tomatoes
- 1 onion, finely chopped
- 1–2 cloves garlic, peeled, crushed and finely chopped
- 10 ml/2 teaspoons pure vegetable oil
- 1–2 tablespoons tomato purée
- 1 tablespoon fresh (or frozen) basil, or 1 teaspoon dried mixed herbs
- pinch sugar
- a little salt and freshly ground black pepper

For the Topping:
- 50–75 g/2–3 oz mozzarella, or low-fat cheddar cheese, grated
- fresh parsley or basil
- choose from the following: red, green or yellow peppers, mushrooms, ham, cooked chicken, or any combination

Preparation:	15 minutes
Cooking:	10 minutes
Freezing:	no
Serves:	2 as a main meal, 4 as a light meal

What you do:

In a heavy saucepan heat the oil. Add the onion and cook gently until soft; add the garlic and cook for one minute. Add the tomatoes, sugar, tomato purée, salt and black pepper. Raise the heat and cook until sufficient water has been driven off to make the sauce a thick purée.

Split the focaccia carefully in two. Lightly toast under a grill. Spread half the sauce on each piece, making sure you spread it right to the edge. Evenly divide your chosen topping — again right to the edge. Finally, sprinkle the grated cheese on top. Place on a baking sheet and bake at 200°C/400°F/Gas 6. You may need to turn the sheet round halfway through to ensure even cooking. If necessary, give the cheese an extra browning under a hot grill. Sprinkle with the chopped parsley and serve hot with a green salad.

Per Serving	(main meal)	(light meal)
Calories	1,238 kcal	621 kcal
Fat	47 g	24 g
Saturated Fat	10.4 g	3.6 g
Fibre	10.8 g	5.4 g

Pasta, Rice, Couscous & Noodles

Summer Vegetables
with Rice

This vegetable dish has strong Mediterranean flavours. It's delicious eaten in the garden.

What you need:

- 200 g/½ lb mange-tout
- 12 pitted black olives
- 350 g/12 oz tomatoes
- 1 red pepper, deseeded
- 4 sun-dried tomatoes, sliced and drained (optional)
- 225 g/8 oz mixed wild and long-grain rice
- 450–600 ml/¾–1 pint vegetable stock
- 15 ml/1 tablespoon olive oil
- 1 clove garlic, crushed
- a little salt and freshly ground black pepper

Preparation:	15 minutes
Cooking:	20 minutes
Freezing:	no
Serves:	4

What you do:

Trim the mange-tout and blanch in boiling water until barely tender. Drain and refresh in cold running water; drain well. Halve the olives and dice the fresh and sun-dried tomatoes, if using. Slice the red pepper into long strips. Put the rice and stock into a saucepan. Bring to the boil, lower the heat and simmer, covered, for about 20 minutes or until all the liquid has been absorbed and the rice is tender. Heat the oil in a large pan or wok. Add the garlic and peppers and cook for 2–3 minutes.

Add the tomatoes and the rice. Cook, stirring over a gentle heat for 3–4 minutes. Stir in the vegetables and olives. Increase the heat and cook, stirring for one minute until piping hot. Season with a little salt and freshly ground black pepper to taste and serve immediately with crusty bread.

Per Serving	
Calories	304 kcal
Fat	8 g
Saturated Fat	1 g
Fibre	3.4 g

Tabouleh Salad

A delicious accompaniment to any meal. Bulgar wheat and couscous are grains used traditionally in Eastern cuisine and are rich in carbohydrates, very low in fat, so ideal 'filler' foods.

What you need:

- 175 g/6 oz Bulgar wheat
- 6 sun-dried tomatoes, finely chopped
- 2 cloves garlic, peeled and chopped
- 1–2 courgettes, or 1 red pepper
- 4–5 tablespoons fresh herbs, choose from mint, chives, parsley or basil, chopped
- juice of 1 lemon
- 30 ml/2 tablespoons olive oil
- 1 red onion, peeled and sliced into thin rings
- black olives, pitted (optional)

Preparation:	10 minutes
Cooking:	10 minutes
Freezing:	no
Serves:	4–6

What you do:

Place the Bulgar wheat in a large bowl, cover with boiling water, and allow it to soak for 10 minutes. Wash, then cut the courgette(s) into small dice. If using a pepper, half, deseed, remove the pith, then cut into small dice. Heat half a tablespoon of the oil in a pan and cook the courgette(s) or pepper over a high heat until they begin to brown. Add the garlic and cook briefly, but do not allow to brown. Drain the Bulgar wheat and squeeze with your hands to remove any excess moisture. Place in a large serving bowl. Mix in the cooked vegetables, the herbs, sun-dried tomatoes, lemon juice and the rest of the olive oil. Garnish with the red onion and olives.

Per Serving	(if serving 6)	(if serving 4)
Calories	186 kcal	279 kcal
Fat	8.3 g	13 g
Saturated Fat	1.06 g	1.6 g
Fibre	0.5 g	0.8g

Spaghetti Alla Puttanesca

Even if you don't like anchovies, try this delicious sauce as you don't really get an anchovy taste. Remember, the healthiest way to eat pasta is like the Italians — lots of pasta and just a little sauce.

What you need:

- 400 g/14 oz dried spaghetti
- ½ medium onion, finely chopped
- 1 red chilli, deseeded and finely chopped
- 2 cloves garlic, chopped
- 400 g/14 oz can chopped tomatoes
- 1 x 50 g/2 oz tin anchovy fillets, drained and chopped
- 15 ml/1 tablespoon olive oil
- 50–100 g/2–4 oz pitted black olives, sliced
- 1 tablespoon small capers, drained
- 4 tablespoons basil/parsley, chopped
- 25–50 g/1–2 oz fresh Parmesan, grated
- a little salt and freshly ground black pepper

Preparation:	10–15 minutes
Cooking:	15–20 minutes
Freezing:	no
Serves:	3–4

What you do:

Cook the pasta according to the packet instructions.

Heat the oil in a heavy-based saucepan and add the onions, chilli and garlic. Cook for 1–2 minutes until the onion is soft and clear. Add the tomatoes and anchovies and cook for 2–3 minutes, stirring occasionally. Add the olives and capers and continue to cook for about 15 minutes. Drain the pasta and add to the sauce. Toss well together and serve in bowls topped with basil or parsley and a little freshly grated or thin curls/slices of Parmesan, if desired.

Per Serving	(if serving 3)	(if serving 4)
Calories	700 kcal	526 kcal
Fat	20 g	15 g
Saturated Fat	4.9 g	3.7 g
Fibre	6.5 g	4.9 g

Spicy Chorizo Pasta

The small amount of chorizo added to this chilli and peppers mixture gives this dish a really spicy flavour. Pasta, like rice and potatoes, is rich in starch, low in fat and calories and very filling.

What you need:

- 350 g/12 oz penne
- 3 red peppers, deseeded and cut into strips
- 1 red chilli, deseeded and finely chopped
- 1 large onion, thinly sliced
- 2 cloves garlic, crushed
- 2 x 400 g/14 oz cans chopped tomatoes
- 15 ml/1 tablespoon olive oil
- 50 g/2 oz thinly sliced chorizo, or salami
- 1 slice brown bread, made into crumbs
- 2 tablespoons fresh parsley/basil, chopped
- 50 g/2 oz fresh Parmesan, grated
- a little salt and freshly ground black pepper

Preparation:	15 minutes
Cooking:	25–30 minutes
Freezing:	no
Serves:	4

What you do:

Pre-heat the oven to 200°C/400°F/Gas 6. Heat the oil in a pan and cook the chilli, peppers and onions for 10 minutes until soft and golden, stirring occasionally. Stir in the garlic and cook for 1 minute. Add the tomatoes, heat through and season. Meanwhile, cook the pasta according to the packet instructions. Drain well and mix with the sauce and chorizo. Spoon into a greased, large, shallow ovenproof dish. Mix together the breadcrumbs, parsley/basil and Parmesan, then sprinkle over the pasta and bake for 15–20 minutes until golden. Serve with crusty garlic bread (see page 107).

Note: For a vegetarian main dish, omit the meat and add one can of beans or chickpeas, drained and rinsed, to the sauce.

Per Serving	
Calories	524 kcal
Fat	13.2 g
Saturated Fat	4.6 g
Fibre	6.5 g

▼ Mango and Chilli Quesadillas (page 73)

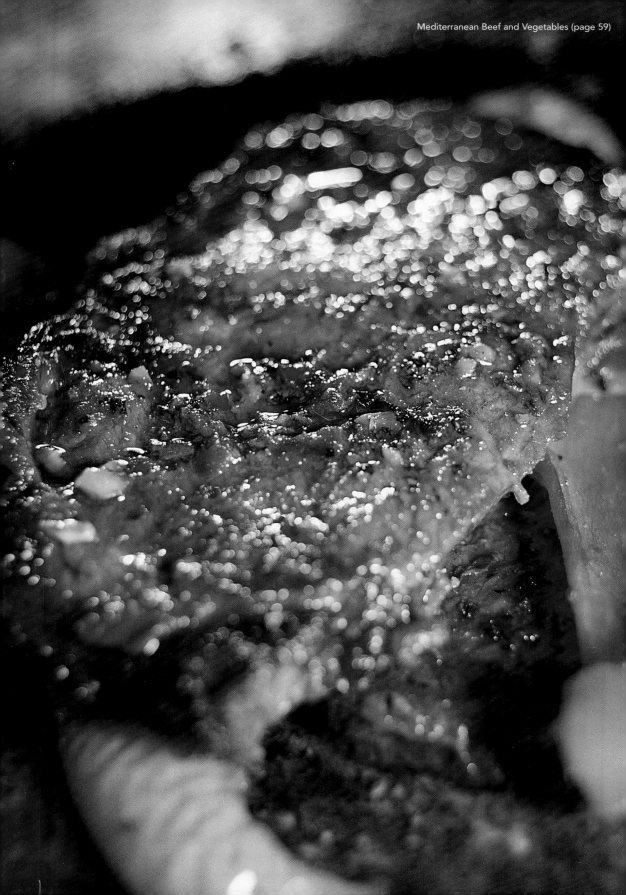

▼ Salmon with Lime, Ginger and Coriander Parcel (page 52)

Tagliatelle with Smoked Haddock

Low-fat crème fraîche gives this dish a deceptively creamy flavour — yet keeps the fat content low. Smoked fish and pasta work very well together.

What you need:

- 1 medium fillet smoked haddock
- 100 g/4 oz dried tagliatelle
- 150 g/5 oz/½ tub low-fat crème fraîche
- 1 clove garlic, crushed
- ½ small onion, finely chopped
- grated zest of 1 lemon
- small handful chopped parsley
- 8 ml/½ tablespoon olive oil
- a little salt and freshly ground black pepper

Preparation:	20 minutes
Cooking:	15 minutes
Freezing:	no
Serves:	2

What you do:

Bring a large pan of water to the boil. Meanwhile, place the haddock in a microwave dish, cover and microwave on high until heated through. Remove, discard the skin, then flake the flesh into large pieces. Add the tagliatelle to the boiling water and cook following the instructions on the packet. Put the oil into a saucepan and gently brown the onion and garlic. Remove the pan from the heat and very gently stir in the lemon rind, parsley and crème fraîche. Drain the tagliatelle and divide between two bowls. Spoon over the sauce. Garnish with more parsley. Serve with lemon wedges, brown bread or brown scones and a green salad.

Per Serving	
Calories	320 kcal
Fat	19 g
Saturated Fat	10 g
Fibre	0.3 g

Pasta Carbonara

A true Italian carbonara does not actually have any cream in it at all, yet the sauce coats the pasta and tastes delicious. Try it — you will be pleasantly surprised!

What you need:
- 500 g/1 lb 2 oz dried spaghetti
- 200 g/7 oz lean smoked back rashers
- 3 cloves garlic, peeled and halved
- 15 ml/1 tablespoon olive oil
- 3 large free range eggs
- 75–100 g/3–4 oz Parmesan or Regato, *plus* a little extra for serving
- freshly ground black pepper

Preparation:	15 minutes
Cooking:	12–15 minutes
Freezing:	no
Serves:	4–5

What you do:
Cook the pasta according to the instructions on the packet. While the pasta cooks, heat a large saucepan and add the olive oil and the garlic and fry until golden. Take it out and discard it. Add the rashers to the flavoured oil and fry them until they start to crisp. Turn off the heat. Beat the eggs in a bowl, grate the cheese finely and stir it into the eggs with plenty of freshly ground black pepper. When the pasta is still a little bit underdone, turn the heat on low under the saucepan of rashers to reheat them. Take out a mugful of the pasta cooking water and keep it. Drain the pasta, leaving it glistening, and return it to the still hot cooking pot. Add the egg and cheese mix plus a little of the pasta water from the mug. Toss well, adding more pasta water if necessary (you would need a total of 50–120 ml/2–4 fl oz). The heat of the water and the pasta cooks the egg lightly but do not reheat or the egg will scramble. Toss the rasher strips through the pasta, adding the garlic-flavoured oil. Serve at once on hot plates with a little more cheese and plenty of freshly ground black pepper.

Note: As with all lightly cooked egg dishes, be sure to use eggs from a quality assured source.

Recipe by Maureen Tatlow. Taken from the National Healthy Eating campaign 1999, Health Promotion Unit.

Per Serving	(if serving 4)	(if serving 5)
Calories	749 kcal	599 kcal
Fat	28 g	22 g
Saturated Fat	10 g	8 g
Fibre	3.75 g	3 g

Spicy Curry Couscous

Couscous is an interesting alternative to rice or pasta and, like Bulgar wheat, easily takes up the flavour of herbs, spices or garlic, making a delicious, flavourful dish.

What you need:

- 250 g/9 oz pre-steamed couscous
- 325 ml/11 fl oz vegetable stock
- 30 ml/2 tablespoons olive oil
- 3 cloves garlic, peeled and sliced
- 1 red pepper, deseeded and diced
- 3 tablespoons mild curry paste
- 1 tablespoon light soy sauce
- 4 tablespoons mango chutney
- 75 g/3 oz sultanas
- 5 tablespoons scallions, chopped
- ½ a cucumber, deseeded and chopped
- zest and juice of 1 lemon

Preparation:	10 minutes
Cooking:	10 minutes
Freezing:	no
Serves:	4

What you do:

Bring 275 ml/9 fl oz of the vegetable stock to the boil. Add the couscous and simmer for one minute, stirring all the time. Remove from the heat; cover, and allow to stand for 4 minutes. Meanwhile, heat the oil in a casserole, then soften (but do not brown) the garlic and the red pepper. Add the curry paste and cook for one minute. Now add the remaining stock, the soy sauce, chutney and sultanas. Bring back to boiling point. Take off the heat and add the lemon juice. Uncover the couscous, fluff up with a fork and stir in the spicy mixture, mixing well. Tip out on to a heated serving dish and garnish with the cucumber, scallions and lemon zest. Serve at once if it is to be eaten warm — although this is also good cold.

Note: Almost all couscous sold in Ireland has been pre-steamed and only requires to be soaked and reheated until hot through.

Per Serving	
Calories	400 kcal
Fat	14.3 g
Saturated Fat	1.1 g
Fibre	1.2 g

Vegetables

Spinach Catalan Style

For spinach lovers, this is a delicious dish. The anchovies add a kick but, strangely, no actual taste of anchovies — so even if you are not an anchovy fan, do give this dish a try.

What you need:

- 2 kg/4½ lb fresh spinach or 450 g/1lb frozen en branche
- 2 cloves garlic, peeled and finely chopped
- 6 anchovy fillets, finely chopped
- 50 g/2 oz pine kernels
- 50 g/2 oz raisins
- 15 ml/1 tablespoon olive oil
- a little salt and freshly ground black pepper

Preparation:	7 minutes
Cooking:	18 minutes
Freezing:	no
Serves:	4

What you do:

Wash the spinach; remove any large stalks. Drop into a large pot of fast-boiling water and boil for 3 minutes. Drain, refresh with cold water. Drain again, pressing out all the water and chop roughly. If using frozen spinach, you will need to squeeze it thoroughly after thawing to remove the copious amount of water that will be present, then chop roughly.

Heat the oil in a wide pan; add the garlic, anchovies, pine kernels, raisins and spinach. Cook gently, stirring frequently with a wooden spoon, for 12–15 minutes. Toss in the spinach, cook for 1–2 minutes, stirring well. Season to taste and serve hot.

Note: Frozen chopped spinach can be used, but it will not give the texture needed for this classic dish, as it is too finely chopped.

Per Serving	
Calories	292 kcal
Fat	14 g
Saturated Fat	1.6 g
Fibre	11 g

Baked Beetroot with Low-fat Crème Fraîche

This is an ideal vegetable to cook with baked potatoes, as medium beetroots take roughly the same time to cook as a large baked potato. Left-over baked beetroots can be transformed into a salad by slicing thinly, topping with a few chopped scallions, a little vinaigrette dressing and chopped fresh parsley.

What you need:

- 4–8 (depending on size) equal-sized, uncooked baby beetroots
- 1 x 200 ml/7 fl oz tub low-fat crème fraîche

Preparation:	5 minutes
Cooking:	1–1½ hours (depending on size)
Freezing:	no
Serves:	4

What you do:

Choose firm, equal-sized beetroots no larger than a tennis ball. Wash well, nip off excess root and leaves but be sure to leave part of the root and leaf stalk intact (to prevent bleeding). Wrap them loosely in tin foil and bake at 200°C/400°F/Gas 6 until tender. Test by squeezing gently. When cooked they should feel soft and slightly squashy. The simplest way to serve them is in their foil packets on a side plate, allowing each person to peel his own beetroot. A garnish of a dessert spoonful of low-fat crème fraîche adds a pleasing flavour that contrasts with the natural sweetness of beetroot.

Per Serving
Calories	129 kcal
Fat	9.6 g
Saturated Fat	6.25 g
Fibre	1.3 g

Curried Cauliflower

There are many ways of adding zest to a rather bland cauliflower from sprinkling it with toasted almonds or, in the Polish way, with sieved hard boiled egg, chopped parsley and toasted breadcrumbs, but one of the tastiest is with a curry flavour and some surprising additions.

What you need:

- 1 fairly large cauliflower
- 225 g/8 oz cooked potato, peeled and diced
- 30 ml/2 tablespoons vegetable oil
- 1 tablespoon mild or medium curry paste
- 3 tablespoons raisins
- 1 large ripe banana, thickly sliced

Preparation:	5 minutes
Cooking:	10 minutes
Freezing:	no
Serves:	4–6

What you do:

Break the cauliflower into florets, discarding the stalk and any leaves. Blanch in boiling water for 3 minutes and drain well. Heat the oil in a saucepan and cook the curry paste briefly until the mixture is smooth and strongly scented. Add the potatoes and cauliflower and stir-fry until lightly coated with paste. Add the bananas and raisins with a splash of water. Cover and shake gently over a moderate heat for 2 minutes, until the cauliflower is just tender. Check the flavour and add freshly milled pepper or a dash of lemon juice if desired. Serve as an accompaniment to chicken or fish, with a little garlic naan bread.

Note: This is a mild version: if a hotter dish is preferred, increase the amount of curry paste. The banana could be omitted, but it adds a nicely rounded flavour.

Per Serving	(if serving 4)	(if serving 6)
Calories	220 kcal	147 kcal
Fat	8.9 g	5.9 g
Saturated Fat	0.6 g	0.4 g
Fibre	3.6 g	2.4 g

Broccoli with Tomato and Orange Sauce

Try this dish for an interesting flavour. Broccoli and cauliflower have special properties thought to be important in helping to prevent cancer — so enjoy them weekly at least!

What you need:

- 1 kg/2 lb broccoli, trimmed

For the Sauce:

- 675 g/1½ lb ripe tomatoes
- 2 tablespoons shallots, finely chopped
- 15 ml/1 tablespoon olive oil
- 1 teaspoon fresh orange juice
- 2 tablespoons parsley, chopped

For the Topping:

- grated rind of 1 orange
- 1 clove garlic, crushed
- 2 tablespoons parsley, chopped

Preparation:	15 minutes
Cooking:	10 minutes
Freezing:	no
Serves:	4–6

What you do:

Cut off the broccoli florets. Pare the stems with a vegetable parer or sharp knife. Cut across in thin slices into julienne strips. Set aside.

Make up the sauce by combining all the ingredients in a bowl. Chop the parsley, garlic and orange rind together for the topping.

Cook the broccoli in boiling water for 3–4 minutes until just tender. Drain and put into a hot vegetable dish. Pour on the tomato mixture, sprinkle with the topping and serve at once to get the contrast of the hot and cold.

Per Serving	(if serving 4)	(if serving 6)
Calories	149 kcal	99.5 kcal
Fat	6.5 g	4.3 g
Saturated Fat	1.2 g	0.8 g
Fibre	8.5 g	5.6 g

Celeriac and Carrot Purée

Celeriac is a knobbly root vegetable that tastes of celery. It naturally contains a lot of water and so puréed, it can be rather wet; this is why it is normally combined with another, dryer vegetable. This is a handy dinner party dish as it can be made ahead of time and reheated in a microwave until hot through.

What you need:

- 300 g/11 oz celeriac (peeled weight)
- 300 g/11 oz carrots (peeled weight)
- 4–6 gratings nutmeg (or pinch of ground nutmeg)
- 30 ml/2 tablespoons light cream (optional)
- a little salt and freshly ground black pepper

Preparation:	8 minutes
Cooking:	20 minutes
Freezing:	no
Serves:	4

What you do:

Choose a firm root of celeriac; peel it, taking care to remove any 'eyes'. Cut into slices about 2 cm/1 inch thick. Peel the carrots and cut into similar-sized pieces. Place both in a pot of boiling water and cook until quite soft — about 20 minutes. Drain and, while still hot, purée in a food processor. Add grated nutmeg, salt and pepper, and cream. Serve hot.

Note: An alternative is to replace the carrots with an equal quantity of floury potatoes. If using potatoes, use a mouli-sieve instead of a food processor as this results in a 'gummy' texture.

Per Serving (without the cream)

Calories	40 kcal
Fat	0.6 g
Saturated Fat	0.08 g
Fibre	4.6 g

Stir-fry Carrots and Cabbage

Dark green leafy vegetables like cabbage and spinach are rich in heart-healthy vitamins. Try to include them two or three times a week.

What you need:

- 750 g/1½ lb green cabbage
- 100 g/4 oz carrots
- 15 ml/1 tablespoon pure vegetable oil
- 2 teaspoons dry sherry or rice wine
- 2 teaspoons soy sauce
- a little salt and freshly ground black pepper, and sugar to taste

Preparation:	10 minutes
Cooking:	10–12 minutes
Freezing:	no
Serves:	5

What you do:

Discard any very coarse outer leaves from the cabbage. Cut out the coarse stalks from the centre of the leaves and roll them up tightly in bundles. Cut across into fine shreds. Blanch in boiling water for one minute, and refresh under cold water. Shake dry in a salad spinner. Chill until required.

Pare the carrots and either cut into julienne strips or pare lengthways into very thin slices.

Heat a wok, add the oil and when it becomes hot, add the carrots and stir-fry for about a minute, then sprinkle with a light seasoning of salt, pepper and sugar. Add the blanched cabbage and mix well. Add the sherry or rice wine. Stir-fry for 3 to 4 minutes until the cabbage is beginning to wilt. Toss with the soy sauce and serve very hot.

Per Serving
Calories   94 kcal
Fat   4.6 g
Saturated Fat   0.4 g
Fibre   5.1 g

Desserts

Frozen Raspberry Yoghurt

This delicious low-calorie dessert is really refreshing, ideal after a 'rich' meal. Raspberries are rich in vitamin C, an antioxidant vitamin that helps protect against heart disease.

What you need:

- 500 g/16 oz raspberries, fresh or frozen
- sugar to taste
- a little water
- 750 ml/1¼ pints natural yoghurt
- a few mint leaves to garnish

Preparation:	5 minutes *plus* about 3 hours freezing
Cooking:	5 minutes
Freezing:	yes
Serves:	4

What you do:

Heat the raspberries in a little water in a saucepan. Alternatively, microwave. When hot, add the sugar to taste and blend into a purée. Put aside a quarter of the purée to serve as a sauce with the frozen yoghurt. Mix the rest of the purée with the natural yoghurt and put in the freezer for approximately 30 minutes. Remove from the freezer, mix thoroughly and put the frozen yoghurt into serving moulds or containers. Put back into the freezer until ready to use. Approximately 30 minutes before serving, transfer the frozen yoghurt to the fridge. Just before serving, heat up the purée and spoon out a little of the sauce on to serving plates. Turn out the frozen yoghurt on to the plates and top with mint leaves.

Note: For a smoother mixture, sieve the raspberry purée to remove the pips. Blackberries can be used instead of raspberries, or thawed frozen fruits in winter.

Per Serving	
Calories	142 kcal
Fat	1.9 g
Saturated Fat	1 g
Fibre	4 g

Winter Fruit Compote

A winter fruit compote made from the last of the season's peaches, pears, plums or any other fresh fruit available is a welcome reminder of summer. Dried fruits such as apricots, figs and prunes can also be used. Try it as a delicious breakfast treat at weekends.

What you need:

- 350 g/12 oz peaches, peeled, halved, stoned and sliced
- 100 g/4 oz plums, halved and stoned
- 100 g/4 oz figs (optional)
- grated rind and juice of 2 small oranges
- water
- 1 tablespoon light brown sugar
- 1 teaspoon mixed spice

Preparation:	20 minutes
Cooking:	10–12 minutes
Freezing:	yes
Serves:	4

What you do:

Soften the prepared fruits by cooking with the orange rind and juice plus sufficient water to make the liquid up to 225 ml/8 fl oz for 10–12 minutes. Combine the sugar and spice, stir into the fruit and leave to cool for 10–15 minutes. Eat hot, or chill before serving.

Serve with natural yoghurt or low-fat crème fraîche.

Note: If using dried fruits, substitute ready-to-eat dried apricots for the fresh peaches and/or stoned prunes. Add chunky slices of banana instead of the plums and warm through just before serving.

Per Serving	
Calories	66 kcal
Fat	0.5 g
Saturated Fat	0.2 g
Fibre	2 g

▼ Seared Tuna with Mexican Salsa (page 51)

◀ Roasted Peppers with Fennel and Garlic (page 31)

▼ Spaghetti Alla Puttanesca (page 81)

◀ Back: Tzatziki (page 44); Front left: Spicy Red Pepper Salsa (page 45); Front right: Basil and Parsley Dressing (page 42)

▼ Sunshine Tomato Salad with Toasted Heart Croutons (page 41)

▲ Spinach Catalan Style (page 89)

Apple and Blackberry Filo Parcels

These apple and blackberry parcels look good and taste delicious. In early autumn why not spend a Saturday afternoon in the country picking fresh blackberries from the hedgerows and use them for Sunday dessert.

What you need:

- 4 sheets filo pastry, thawed
- 25 g/1 oz unsalted butter, melted
- 8 ml/½ tablespoon pure vegetable oil
- icing sugar for dusting

Preparation:	20 minutes
Cooking:	about 8–10 minutes
Freezing:	no
Serves:	4

For the Filling:

- 4 large apples, peeled, cored and cut into slices
- 225 g/8 oz large blackberries
- 50 g/2 oz caster sugar
- 13 g/½ oz butter
- a squeeze of lemon juice
- a pinch of ground cinnamon
- pouring custard made on low-fat milk or natural yoghurt

What you do:

Pre-heat the oven to 200°C/400°F/Gas 6. To make the filling, heat a large heavy-based pan, add the butter and once it is melted, toss in the apples and a squeeze of lemon juice. Cook for 3 minutes, turning occasionally until lightly golden. Sprinkle over sugar and cinnamon and continue to cook until the apples are caramelised. Add the blackberries and toss until just warmed through. Leave to cool. Place the pastry sheets on a baking tray and brush lightly with the melted butter. In the centre of each filo sheet, make a little fruit pile and twist the pastry together at the top to make a little parcel (like an old-fashioned draw string money bag). Transfer into the oven and bake for 8–10 minutes or until crisp and golden brown.

To serve, arrange the filo parcel in the middle of the plate and pour any juices remaining from stewing the fruit in a circle around the filo parcel. Serve at once. Low-fat custard made with low-fat milk can be offered as an accompaniment, or a spoonful of natural/Greek yoghurt.

Per Serving	
Calories	249 kcal
Fat	10.4 g
Saturated Fat	5.5 g
Fibre	7 g

Rhubarb and Orange Yoghurt Fool

Adding orange zest to rhubarb gives it a really delicious flavour. For a quick, easy and tasty summer dessert, this one is hard to beat!

What you need:

- 700 g/1½ lb rhubarb, cut into 1 inch cubes
- 50–75 g/2–3 oz caster sugar
- grated rind and juice of 1 large orange
- 1 x 200 ml tub/7 fl oz Greek yoghurt

Preparation:	5 minutes
Cooking:	3–5 minutes *microwave*
	30 minutes *regular oven*
Freezing:	yes
Serves:	3–4

What you do:

Place the rhubarb, caster sugar, orange juice and rind in a microwave-proof dish. Cover and microwave on 'high' for 3–5 minutes until soft; or bake in a covered ovenproof dish for about 30 minutes at 180°C/350°F/Gas 4, until tender. Leave to cool. Make into a purée in a blender, adding the yoghurt gradually. Serve garnished with a slice of orange and a little grated orange zest.

Per Serving	(if serving 3)	(if serving 4)
Calories	180 kcal	135 kcal
Fat	6.6 g	5 g
Saturated Fat	3.5 g	2.6 g
Fibre	3.3 g	2.5 g

Raspberry and Cinnamon Meringues

These little meringues look and taste delicious. They are very low in fat and not too high in calories. Raspberries are rich in vitamin C so you're doing your heart some good too!

What you need:

- 25 g/1 oz brown breadcrumbs
- ½ teaspoon ground cinnamon, or ½ teaspoon grated orange or lemon rind
- 225 g/8 oz raspberries
- 75 g/3 oz light brown sugar
- 2 egg whites

Preparation:	10 minutes
Cooking:	15–20 minutes
Freezing:	no
Serves:	4

What you do:

Preheat the oven to 190°C/375°F/Gas 5. Put the breadcrumbs on to a baking sheet, sprinkle with cinnamon and grill under a low heat for 30–60 seconds until toasted and crisp. Remove from the heat. Whisk the egg whites into stiff peaks. Continue whisking, adding about half the sugar until the mixture is stiff and glossy. Fold in the remaining sugar. Add the raspberries to the breadcrumb mixture and lightly fold into the meringue. Spoon into four 8 cm/3 inch ramekins. Bake for 15–20 minutes until golden. Serve in the ramekins.

Per Serving
Calories   101 kcal
Fat   0.3 g
Saturated Fat   0.3 g
Fibre   2 g

Hot Mango, Banana and Fruit Salad

Mango gives this quick and easy dessert an exotic flavour. All fruits are fat free and low in calories. Have at least four servings of fruit and vegetables every day.

What you need:

- 2 large oranges
- 2 ripe mangoes (about 700 g/1½ lb), peeled
- 4 small bananas, peeled
- 25 g/1 oz butter
- 1 teaspoon light brown sugar
- 2 tablespoons rum (optional) or 1 teaspoon ground cinnamon
- 2 tablespoons lemon juice

Preparation:	15 minutes
Cooking:	5 minutes
Freezing:	no
Serves:	4

What you do:

Thinly pare the rind from one orange and squeeze the juice. Cut the pared rind into very thin strips and blanch in boiling water for one minute and drain. Set the rind and juice aside, peel the other orange with a serrated knife and slice the flesh crosswise into rounds. Cut the mango flesh into bite-size pieces. Thickly slice the bananas.

Melt the butter in a large non-stick saucepan. Add the sugar, mango and banana and brown for 2–3 minutes. Pour in the rum, if using, or cinnamon, lemon juice and the orange juice. Add the orange slices. Bring to the boil very gently. Serve immediately topped with orange rind.

Per Serving	
Calories	184 kcal
Fat	5.4 g
Saturated Fat	3.4 g
Fibre	3.5 g

Mixed Red Berry Sorbet

Another delicious, refreshing dessert. Make this during the summer and freeze — a great way to enjoy summer fruits in the winter time.

What you need:

- 450 g/1 lb mixed raspberries and strawberries
- 100 g/4 oz caster sugar
- 600 ml/1 pint water
- 3 tablespoons lemon juice
- mint leaves to garnish

Preparation:	15 minutes and about 3 hours freezing
Cooking:	none
Freezing:	yes
Serves:	8

What you do:

Remove the stalks from the berries and rinse them in cold water. Drain well and dry them on kitchen paper before putting them into a food processor. Blend them to a smooth purée. Sieve to remove raspberry pips, return the mixture to the blender, add the sugar, water and lemon juice, and blend until smooth again.

Pour the mixture into a polythene freezer box, cover with the lid and put into the freezer for 2 hours.

After 2 hours the mixture should have started to freeze around the sides and base of the container. Beat until well mixed, cover and return to the freezer for another hour. At this stage the mixture should be completely frozen and ready to serve. Garnish with mint leaves.

Per Serving	
Calories	63 kcal
Fat	0.17 g
Saturated Fat	0.06 g
Fibre	1.3 g

Breads, Biscuits & Cakes

Lower-fat Garlic Bread

It's easy to make lower-fat garlic bread — just substitute low-fat butter or low-fat spread for full fat. The garlic and herb flavours ensure there's no loss of taste.

What you need:

- 1 French baguette
- 75 g/3 oz low-fat butter or low-fat spread
- handful of fresh parsley, chopped, or 1 teaspoon dried mixed herbs
- 2–3 cloves garlic, crushed — or more if you really like garlic

Preparation:	10 minutes
Cooking:	15 minutes
Freezing:	no
Serves:	6

What you do:

Combine the butter or spread with the garlic, parsley and herbs. Cut across but not completely through the baguette at 2 cm/¾ inch intervals. Spread the garlic mixture evenly between the slices. Cut the baguette into two pieces and wrap each in tin foil. Bake for about 15 minutes and serve hot from the oven.

Note: If you use butter or margarine instead, it doubles the fat content to almost 12 g per serving. Considering this is only an accompaniment, if you make garlic bread regularly, it's worth substituting the low-fat butter or margarine.

Per Serving
Calories   155 kcal
Fat   5.8 g
Saturated Fat   1.4 g
Fibre   0.7 g

Easy Home-made Brown Bread

There are dozens of different recipes for home-made brown bread, some using wholemeal alone, others mixing in plain white flour to lighten it, and others with different grains added. Made with the addition of a little butter, or more recently with a spoonful of olive oil, the bread will keep fresh for a second day or can be frozen successfully.

What you need:

- 450 g/1 lb wholemeal flour, coarse or medium
- 175 g/6 oz plain white flour
- 1 teaspoon salt
- 1 teaspoon bread soda (bicarbonate of soda)
- about 450 ml/¾ pint buttermilk

Optional:

- 15 g/½ oz butter, or 1 tablespoon olive oil
- 1–2 teaspoons soft dark brown sugar

Preparation:	10 minutes
Cooking:	35–40 minutes
Freezing:	yes
Serves:	6–8

What you do:

Put the wholemeal flour in a bowl. Sieve together the plain flour, salt and baking soda over the wholemeal flour and mix lightly. At this stage you may rub in the butter or stir in the oil and add the sugar, if desired. Make a well in the centre of the dry ingredients and pour in about two-thirds of the buttermilk. Mix, then add just enough of the remaining buttermilk to give a relaxed mixture that is not too soft to handle.

Turn the dough out on to a clean surface dusted with wholemeal flour and knead lightly into a ball. Place on a greased and floured baking tray and pat out into a round about 4 cm/1½ inches thick. Cut a cross into the bread and bake (oven pre-heated to 200°C/400°F/Gas 6) for 35 to 40 minutes, until the bread sounds hollow when tapped underneath. Cool, wrapped in a tea towel, on a wire rack.

Note: A wide range of Irish bread mixes are now available — just add water and bake. The mixed grain varieties are rich in fibre and delicious. Also try the spice-flavoured and Mediterranean flavours. If using butter or olive oil, you add at least 2 g of fat per serving.

Recipe by Honor Moore.

Per Serving	with butter and sugar	with olive oil and sugar	plain
Calories	289 kcal	290 kcal	270 kcal
Fat	3.3 g	3.7 g	1.8 g
Saturated Fat	1.4 g	0.7 g	0.4 g
Fibre	5.8 g	5.8 g	5.8 g

Focaccia

Focaccia is a light and versatile flat Italian bread. It can be made with a variety of toppings or used for a pizza base as suggested in the recipe below. While not low in fat, there is no need to add fat to the bread once cooked. It makes it an ideal accompaniment to salads, especially salads using tomatoes or sun-dried tomatoes.

What you need:

- 400 g/14 oz strong, unbleached, white flour
- 2 teaspoons dried yeast (1½ teaspoons fast-action dried yeast)
- 45 ml/3 tablespoons extra virgin olive oil
- 1 teaspoon salt
- about 300 ml/10 fl oz water (hand hot)

For the Flavourings/Toppings:

- 15 ml/1 tablespoon extra virgin olive oil
- a good pinch coarse sea salt
- You may also choose one of the following: 1½ tablespoons fresh, chopped rosemary, thyme or sage, or 8–10 rings of raw onion.

Preparation:	10 minutes *plus* 2–3 hours rising time
Cooking:	20 minutes
Freezing:	no
Serves:	8 wedges

What you do:

If using 'traditional' dried yeast, activate it by mixing with 4 tablespoons of warm water and leave in a warm place for about 5–8 minutes or until it begins to become frothy and bubbles rise when you stir it. If using fast-action yeast, mix it directly into the flour. In a food processor or the bowl of a heavy-duty mixer, place the flour, yeast, olive oil, salt and sufficient warm water to absorb the flour and form a dough. If using a food processor, mix until the dough forms into one or two lumps and rides up on the blades. This will take between 50 seconds and 2 minutes. In a heavy-duty mixer it will take about five minutes (this initial mixing may also be done by hand).* Place the dough on a very lightly floured surface and knead vigorously until all traces of stickiness have left the dough and it feels smooth and silky in your hands. Hand-kneaded dough takes about 10 minutes; dough from a mixer or food processor takes only 1–2 minutes. Place dough in a large lightly oiled bowl and cover — clingfilm is fine.

Leave it to rise in a warm place until it has doubled in size. This takes about 2 hours. Knock down the dough, place on a work surface and knead lightly. If you are incorporating flavourings into the dough, add them now. Roll out either into a rectangle or a circle. It should be about ½–1 inch thick. Place on a lightly oiled baking sheet. Dimple the top of the dough with your fingertips, brush 1 tablespoon of oil over the whole of the top and sprinkle with coarse sea salt. Cover with a damp tea towel and allow to rest for about 10 minutes before baking at 200–220°C/400–425°F/Gas 7 for about 20 minutes. It is cooked when the loaf sounds hollow when tapped lightly on the bottom. Remove from the baking sheet and place on a wire rack. This bread is best eaten while still warm.

Recipe by Biddy White Lennon.

*Note: Some people find kneading dough by hand to be a relaxing, almost therapeutic activity. Why not try it and see!

Per Serving	(if serving 8)
Calories	240 kcal
Fat	8.2 g
Saturated Fat	1.2 g
Fibre	1.6 g

Dough Balls

For a dinner party or special meal, dough balls can be served instead of bread as an accompaniment to an Italian meal. They look good and taste delicious.

What you need:

- 45 g/1½ oz fresh yeast, or 25 g/¾ oz active dried yeast
- 300 ml/½ pint lukewarm water
- 15 ml/1 tablespoon olive oil
- 600 g/1¼ lb plain or strong flour
- 1¼ teaspoons salt

Preparation:	2 hours
Cooking:	7–10 minutes
Freezing:	uncooked dough balls
Serves:	24–30 balls (6–8 servings)

What you do:

Stir the fresh or dried yeast into the lukewarm water and leave to froth up (about 10 minutes). Add the olive oil. Sieve the flour and salt into a large bowl and make a well in the centre. Pour the yeast mixture into the well and gradually work in the flour. Knead for 5 minutes in an electric mixer or 10 minutes by hand on a floured surface. Oil the bowl and turn the dough in it until it is evenly coated. Cover the bowl with clingfilm and set to rise in a warm place until doubled in size (about 1 hour). Turn the dough out and knead lightly. Lightly knead pieces of the dough about the size of walnuts into balls. Set out on greased baking trays, spaced well apart, and leave to rise again until doubled in size. Bake in a hot oven 220°C/425°F/Gas 7 for 5 –10 minutes until beginning to brown. Serve warm from the oven.

Note: The uncooked balls of dough can be open-frozen, then wrapped and stored in the freezer. Thaw and leave to rise before baking.

Per Serving	(4 dough balls)
Calories	290 kcal
Fat	3 g
Saturated Fat	0.4 g
Fibre	2.5 g

Carrot Cake

This special low-fat carrot cake uses prune purée in place of some oil to keep it moist and full of flavour. The spices and carrots make this a delicious cake to share with family and friends.

What you need:

- 225 g/8 oz self-raising flour
- 1½ teaspoons baking powder, sieved
- 1½ teaspoons bread soda, sieved
- 200 g/7 oz carrots, grated
- 50 g/2 oz sultanas
- 75 ml/3 fl oz pure vegetable oil
- 50 g/2 oz prune purée*
- 50 g/2 oz walnuts, chopped
- 1 teaspoon cinnamon
- 1 teaspoon mixed spice
- ½ teaspoon salt
- 3 eggs, beaten
- 100–150 g/4–5 oz brown sugar

Preparation:	30 minutes
Cooking:	1¼–1½ hours
Freezing:	yes un-iced
Serves:	up to 12 slices

What you do:

Mix all the dry ingredients together. Add the carrots, oil, prune purée and beaten eggs and mix well. Transfer to an 8 inch round lightly oiled, base-lined tin. Bake at 180°C/350°F /Gas 4 for 1¼–1½ hours.

*Prune Purée

To make one cup of the prune purée, put 225 g/8 oz of stoned prunes and 90 ml/ 6 tablespoons of hot water in a liquidiser and purée until smooth. Prune purée can be stored in the fridge for up to two months in a tightly sealed jar. This purée can be combined with crème fraîche and grated lemon rind to make a sponge cake filling.

Note: This cake can be eaten without icing, but for a special occasion the following icing turns it into a scrumptious treat.

Per Serving	Per slice of cake without icing
Calories	247 kcal
Fat	11 g
Saturated Fat	1.2 g
Fibre	2.3 g

Carrot Cake Icing

What you need:
- 100 g/4 oz light cream cheese
- 1 teaspoon orange juice (you may need a little extra juice)
- rind of 1 orange, grated
- 225 g/8 oz icing sugar
- 25 g/1 oz walnuts, finely chopped

What you do:
Blend the light cream cheese, orange juice and rind and icing sugar together (this takes a little time to come together). Keep blending. You may need a few extra drops of orange juice, but be careful not to add too much or you will end up with runny icing. Spoon the icing on to the cake and spread with a wet palette knife. Sprinkle with finely chopped walnuts.

Per Serving	Per slice of cake with icing
Calories	343 kcal
Fat	13.7 g
Saturated Fat	2.2 g
Fibre	3.2 g

Banana Cake

This delicious banana cake is low in fat, because banana purée has been used to replace some of the oil. Try it occasionally as a special treat.

What you need:

- 350 g/12 oz self-raising flour
- 1 teaspoon bread soda
- 2 teaspoons mixed spice
- 175 g/6 oz light brown sugar
- 3 large eggs
- 75 ml/3 fl oz sunflower oil
- 2 oz banana purée
- 2 large bananas, mashed
- 75 g/3 oz sultanas
- finely grated rind and juice of 1 orange
- 100 g/4 oz pack walnuts, roughly chopped

For the Filling:

- 1 x 100 g/4 oz pack light cream cheese, at room temperature
- 100 g/4 oz icing sugar
- rind of 1 orange
- 2–3 teaspoons orange juice

Preparation:	20 minutes
Cooking:	45 minutes
Freezing:	yes unfilled
Serves:	12 slices

What you do:

Grease and line 2 x 20 cm/8 inch sandwich tins. Pre-heat the oven to 180°C/350°F/Gas 4. Sieve the flour into a large bowl with the bread soda. Mix the spice and sugar. Whisk the eggs and the oil with a balloon whisk until smooth. Use a large fork to stir into the flour the bananas, sultanas, orange rind, juice and walnuts. Stir well. Divide between the prepared tins. Bake for 45 minutes until risen and firm. Cool for 10 minutes, then remove from the tins. Peel off the paper and leave to cool completely. Put the light cream cheese into a bowl and whisk until smooth. Gradually add the icing sugar to give a smooth filling. Then add the grated orange rind and a little of the orange juice, adding by the half-teaspoon until you get the required texture. Spread the filling over the top of one of the cakes and sandwich together with the other cake. If serving immediately, add a layer of mashed banana for extra flavour.

Per Serving	(slice)
Calories	372 kcal
Fat	15.3 g
Saturated Fat	2.5 g
Fibre	19 g

Bran Muffins

Muffins are a type of quick bread, though higher in fat than traditional breads. They are simple to make. Muffins have been part of the American way of eating for a number of years and when you make your own it is easy to see why.

What you need:
First Bowl:

- 50 g/2 oz wheat bran
- 175 ml/6 fl oz buttermilk
- 1 egg
- 60 ml/4 tablespoons pure vegetable oil
- 50 g/2 oz raisins
- 1 tablespoon treacle
- grated rind of 1 orange (optional)

Second Bowl:

- 100 g/4 oz brown sugar
- 100 g/4 oz plain flour
- 1 teaspoon bread soda, sieved
- 1 teaspoon ground cinnamon

Preparation:	20 minutes
Cooking:	15–20 minutes
Freezing:	yes
Serves:	12 muffins

What you do:
Combine the ingredients in the first bowl and allow to stand for 10 minutes.

Mix together the ingredients in the second bowl. Add the dry ingredients to the wet ingredients, being careful not to overmix. Spoon into lightly oiled muffin or bun tins. Alternatively, line the tins with bun cases. Bake at 180°C/350°F/Gas 4 for 20 minutes.

Note: Wheat bran is sold in most supermarkets now and in many specialist food shops. It is an excellent source of fibre and can be added to muffins, breads, stews or soups for extra fibre.

Per Serving	(1 muffin)
Calories	140 kcal
Fat	5.9 g
Saturated Fat	0.8 g
Fibre	1.9 g

American Apple Muffins

These delicious muffins are dense with apples and raisins. They are very filling and particularly moist. Either cooking or eating apples can be used.

What you need:

- 450 g/1 lb apples, peeled and finely diced
- 150 g/5 oz brown sugar
- 2 eggs, beaten
- 75 ml/3 fl oz vegetable oil
- 100 g/4 oz plain flour
- 100 g/4 oz wholemeal flour
- 2 level teaspoons bread soda, sieved
- 2 level teaspoons ground cinnamon
- 150 g/5 oz raisins
- 75 g/3 oz walnuts, chopped

Preparation:	20 minutes
Cooking:	15–20 minutes
Freezing:	yes
Serves:	18–20 muffins

What you do:

In a large bowl toss together the diced apples and sugar. Add the eggs and oil and mix well. In a second bowl mix together the flours, bread soda and cinnamon. Add the flour mixture to the apple mixture and stir until just combined. Stir in the nuts and raisins. Spoon into the bun or muffin tins that have been lightly oiled or lined with bun cases. Bake for 25 minutes at 180°C/350°F/Gas 4.

Note: It is very important not to overmix when combining the flour and the wet ingredients or when adding the nuts and raisins. Muffins freeze very well. Cool and wrap in aluminium foil or put into freezer bags. Thaw at room temperature.

Per Serving	(1 muffin)
Calories	172 kcal
Fat	7.8 g
Saturated Fat	0.9 g
Fibre	1.4 g

Banana Muffins

This is a delicious way to use up overripe bananas and are a particular favourite with children, for both teatime snacks and lunchtime treats.

What you need:

- 350 g/12 oz bananas, peeled and mashed (2–3 bananas)
- 60 ml/4 tablespoons pure vegetable oil
- 50 ml/2 fl oz low-fat milk
- 1 egg, beaten
- 2 teaspoons baking powder
- 1 teaspoon ground nutmeg
- 50 g/2 oz plain flour
- 150 g/5 oz wholemeal flour
- 50 g/2 oz sugar
- 25 g/1 oz almonds/hazelnuts (optional)

Preparation:	10 minutes
Cooking:	20–25 minutes
Freezing:	yes
Serves:	12–14 muffins

What you do:

Combine the bananas with the oil, milk and egg, mixing well. In a second bowl mix together the remaining ingredients. Add the banana mixture and stir quickly until mixed but still lumpy. Spoon into lightly greased bun or muffin tins. Alternatively, line tins with bun cases.

Bake at 200°C/400°F/Gas 6 for 20–25 minutes.

Muffin recipes are taken from *Cooking for Health* cookery book, Kilkenny Health Project.

Per Serving	(1 muffin)
Calories	164 kcal
Fat	7 g
Saturated Fat	1 g
Fibre	1.7 g

Light Sponge Cake

This delicious and light sponge cake doesn't have any butter, margarine or oil in it — so it's lower in fat than most cakes.

What you need:
- 3 large eggs
- 100 g/4 oz caster sugar
- 75 g/3 oz plain flour
- a few drops vanilla essence or a little grated lemon rind (optional)

For the Filling:
- 4 tablespoons raspberry or apricot jam or liquidised fresh fruit
- 100 ml/4 fl oz low-fat crème fraîche
- a little icing sugar for dusting
- flour and caster sugar for the tins

Preparation:	25 minutes
Cooking:	20–25 minutes
Freezing:	yes, unfilled in a rigid container
Serves:	8

What you do:

Grease and line two 7 inch sandwich tins with baking parchment. Dust with a mixture of flour and caster sugar and discard any excess.

Put the eggs and sugar in a large heatproof bowl and set it over a pan of gently simmering water. Whisk with an electric beater until the mixture has doubled in size and is thick enough to hold the imprint of the whisk. Take the bowl from the heat and whisk for a few minutes more or until the mixture is cool. At this stage you may whisk in a flavouring — a few drops of vanilla extract or grated lemon rind. Sieve half the flour over the surface of the mixture and fold in very lightly, using a large metal spoon. Repeat with the remaining flour and divide the mixture between the two tins. Bake at 190°C/375°F/Gas 5 for 20–25 minutes until golden-brown, firm to the touch and beginning to shrink slightly from the sides of the tin. Turn out on to a wire rack and leave to cool. Strip off the lining paper. Fill with jam or liquidised fresh fruit in season and crème fraîche, and sandwich together. Dust the top with sieved icing sugar.

Per Serving	(1 slice)
Calories	167 kcal
Fat	4.5 g
Saturated Fat	2.2 g
Fibre	0.3 g

Index